Labyrinth Journeys

50 States, 51 Stories

Twylla Alexander

Peace on your path,
Twylla Alexander
2/10/17

2017

ISBN 978-0-692-83499-2

Library of Congress Control Number 2017900857

Original artwork by Margie Beedle
Cover and book design by James Matthews

Grateful acknowledgment is made for permission to reprint the following copyrighted works:

Art from Her Heart: Folk Artist Clementine Hunter by Kathy Whitehead. Copyright © 2008 by Kathy Whitehead. Used by permission of G. P. Putnam's Sons Books for Young Readers (Penguin Random House).

Printed and bound in USA
First Printing January 2017

Published by Springhill Publishing
61 Springhill Drive West
Greenbrier, AR 72058

Visit www.labyrinthjourneys.org

labyrinth a single, circuitous path that leads from entrance to center and back to entrance, with no tricks or dead ends, as in a maze;

a walking meditation;

a journey.

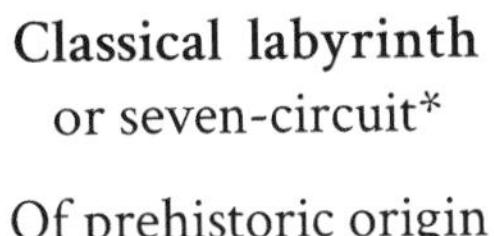

Classical labyrinth
or seven-circuit*

Of prehistoric origin

Chartres labyrinth
or eleven-circuit*

Built into the floor of
Chartres Cathedral in France
1201

* "Seven-circuit" and "eleven-circuit" refer to the number of rings that circle the center.

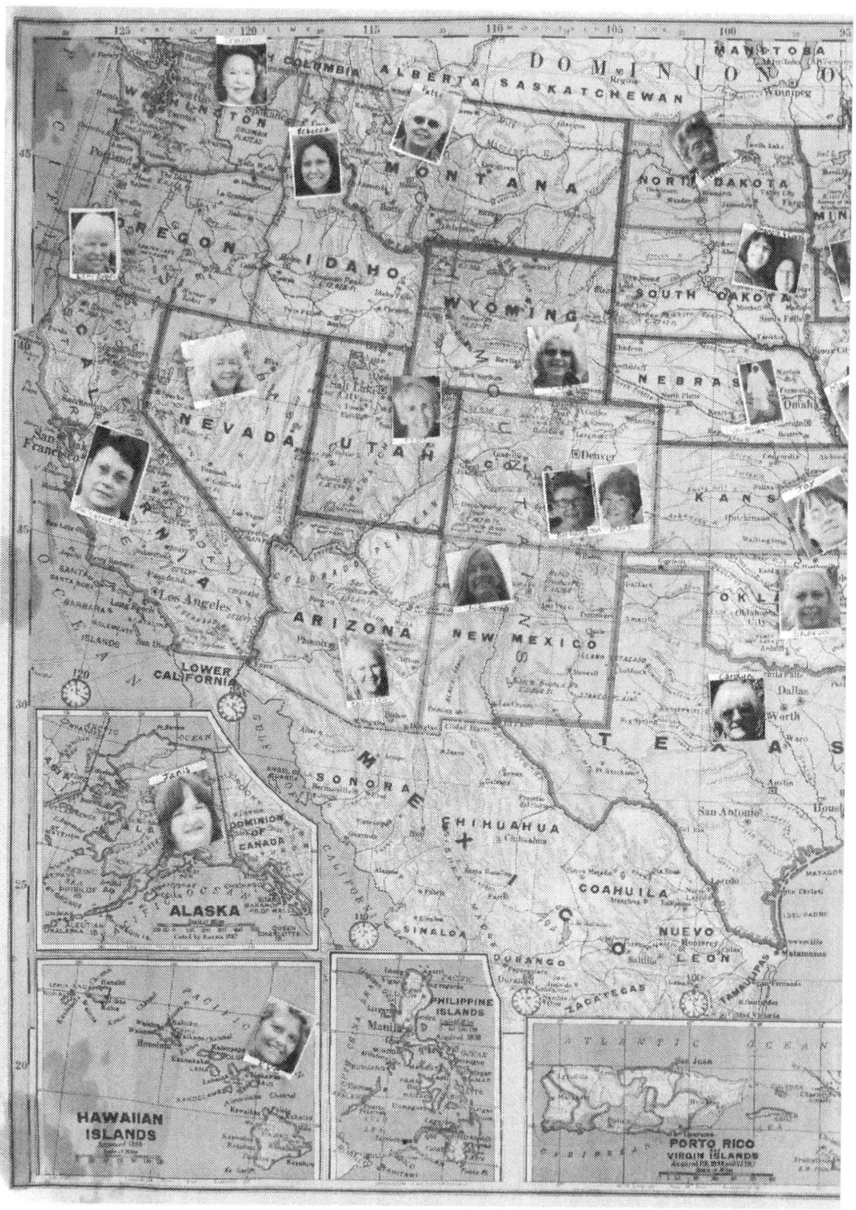

ALBERTA
SASKATCHEWAN
MONTANA
OREGON
IDAHO
WYOMING
SOUTH DAKOTA
NEVADA
UTAH
Denver
Los Angeles
ARIZONA
NEW MEXICO
LOWER CALIFORNIA
SONORA
CHIHUAHUA
COAHUILA
NUEVO LEON
San Antonio
Dallas
ALASKA
DOMINION OF CANADA
HAWAIIAN ISLANDS
PHILIPPINE ISLANDS
PORTO RICO
VIRGIN ISLANDS

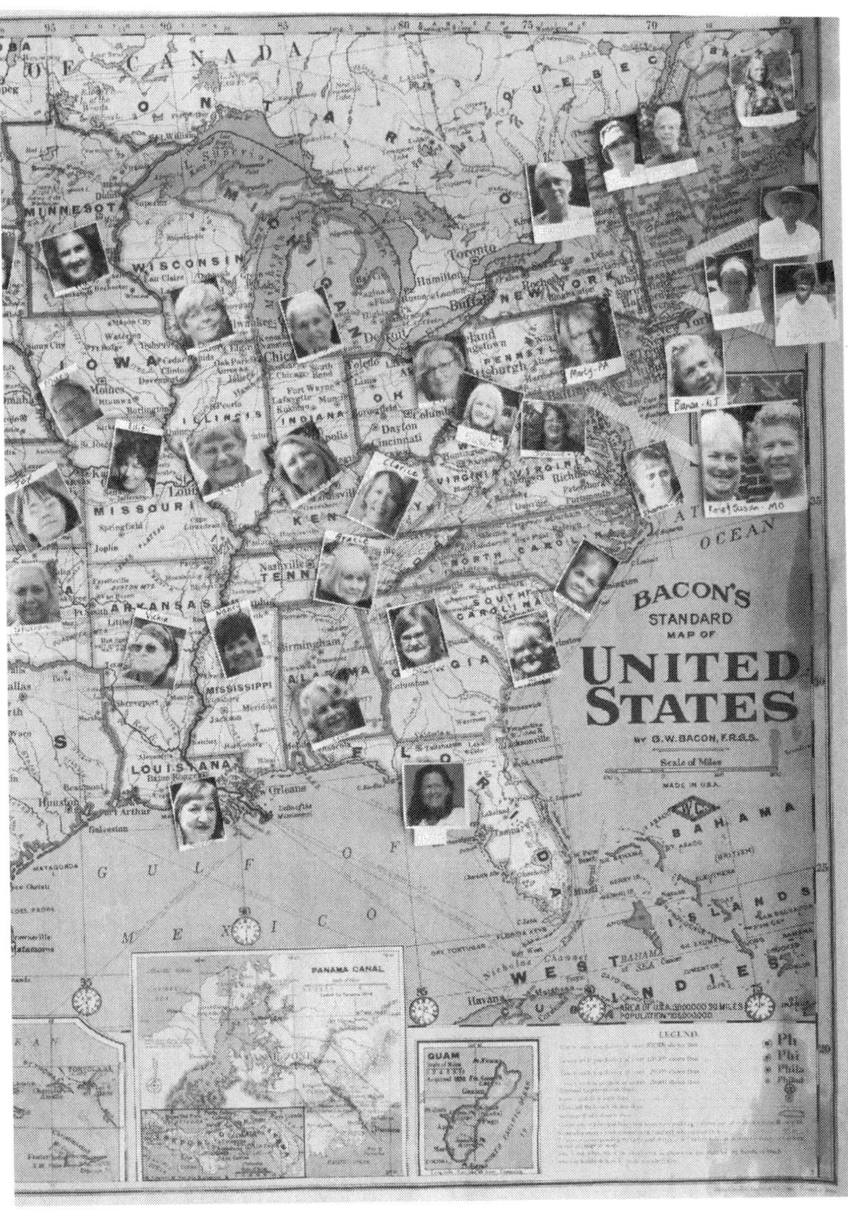
BACON'S
STANDARD
MAP OF
UNITED
STATES
BY G.W. BACON, F.R.G.S.
Scale of Miles
MADE IN U.S.A.
CANADA
ONTARIO
QUEBEC
MINNESOTA
WISCONSIN
MICHIGAN
IOWA
ILLINOIS
INDIANA
OH
MISSOURI
KEN
TENN
ARKANSAS
MISSISSIPPI
ALABAMA
GEORGIA
LOUISIANA
NEW YORK
VIRGINIA
NORTH CAROLINA
SOUTH CAROLINA
FLORIDA
OCEAN
GULF OF MEXICO
BAHAMA ISLANDS
WEST INDIES
PANAMA CANAL
QUAM
LEGEND
Toronto
Chicago
Detroit
Nashville
Birmingham
Orleans
Houston
Havana
Marty-PA
Barbara-NJ
Janet Susan - MD

Contents

For Drew
For Marian and Margie
For fifty women who said, *Yes!*

INTRODUCTION

A Journey in the Making

When I began this two-year journey in 2012, traveling wasn't new to me. After all, I'd already walked a mile on the frozen Arctic Ocean, sped down sand dunes in the Sahara and crept along a Moscow freeway during a snowy, five-hour gridlock; but a pilgrimage to visit fifty states and fifty women who had built their own labyrinths was . . . *personal.*

It was Drew's spirit of adventure that propelled us to pack up our three kids and fifteen suitcases in 1987 and fly from Arkansas to Alaska to teach. Nine years later, the same tempting spirit tapped him on the shoulder and casually whispered, "International teaching, check it out."

I could have said, "No thanks, not interested" anywhere along the way; but frankly, job offerings in Singapore, then Cairo, Moscow, and finally New York City awakened my own imagination for travel and diversity from a deep, predictable sleep.

Inklings for a journey of my own began more subtly, like a leaf that comes to rest on your shoulder during an autumn walk in the woods. You discover it later, press its golden shape in a book, and forget where you put it. But it remains.

It remains as a question, waiting for a reply that can only come from within.

What is *my* journey, my very own journey?

It began with my first labyrinth walk.

July, 2004
Shrine of St. Therese
Juneau, Alaska

My friend Margie and I turned off Glacier Highway at Mile Marker 23 onto a narrow dirt road flanked by evergreens.

"Tomorrow's supposed to be a sunny day," Margie had said when she called the night before. "How about if we take a picnic to the Shrine, walk the labyrinth, then sit on the beach and catch up."

I had been to the Shrine of St. Therese before but had never noticed a labyrinth. In fact I had no idea what a labyrinth was or why Margie thought we should walk it; but wanting to spend time with her, I said, "Sure!"

We ventured down the sloping hill from the parking lot, past the caretaker's cabin and two-story log cabin lodge toward the rocky beach. Waves from the Lynn Canal pulsed in and out as two eagles swooped towards an acrobatic salmon, came up short and argued strategy.

"So, where's the labyrinth?" I asked.

"Behind you," Margie answered turning her head in the direction of the lodge. Had it been any other season besides Juneau's brief summer when Sitka rose bushes, columbine, daisies and a multitude of wildflowers formed a lush border around its perimeter, the labyrinth would have been clearly visible.

I drew closer until circles appeared, circles within circles. I counted eleven of them expanding from a circular center, all outlined with stones from the beach. Turns alternated with curved stretches from one common entrance. A gray boulder sat in the center.

"It's huge," I whispered as we approached a simple brown sign with yellow letters, *Entrance to Merciful Love Prayer Labyrinth.* Even upon first introduction, I felt an urge to lower my voice, as if I had stepped into a library or stood on the threshold of a forest.

"Just start when you're ready and follow the path," Margie said, picking up two shells to carry as she walked.

I watched her circling peacefully from one turn to the next, hands behind her back, eyes on the path. She stopped occasionally to gaze across the water where a humpback whale might surface unexpectedly or toward the tree-covered island where St. Therese stood hidden atop her granite pedestal. I assumed that Margie would eventually reach the boulder in the center, but the path was obviously in no hurry to take her there. One minute she would be inches away, the next headed toward the farthest edge. Perhaps the center was not the goal.

My body knew it was time to begin before my mind caught up. I stepped onto the sandy path, followed it left, right, left, around the center and on. The rhythm of the turns flowed into me as I found my pace and walked where the path would take me. Margie and I touched hands as we passed once, then again minutes later, on the same path but at different places. There was no expectation to catch up, slow down, to pause or stop. I was free to experience my own journey in my own way. It felt like an invitation that the labyrinth had addressed to me. I had no way of knowing how opening the invitation would change my life.

THE LEAF REMAINED pressed in my metaphoric book until the day our son, Jason, handed Drew and me his dog-eared paperback, *A Walk in the Woods* by Bill Bryson.

"Read this," he said. "It'll give you an idea about the journey I'm going to take."

The Appalachian Trail, the longest hiking-only footpath in the world, 2,160 miles from Maine to Georgia.

He would hike for six months, with partners and alone, equipped with a fit body, bulging backpack, sturdy shoes and an open spirit.

Except for bears and black flies, I was intrigued—or more accurately—I was jealous. Each day of Jason's route would be known, could be plotted on a map; but his unique walk was uncertain, to be determined by his choices and encounters. What would he learn about himself? What would he write in his journal each night before falling into an exhausted sleep?

I longed for such a journey that resonated so deeply in me that I would walk every step of the 2,160 miles to experience what I was supposed to experience. I wanted to travel to places I had never been, learn things about myself I had never learned, meet people and hear their stories. It sounded like a journey I had already taken from Arkansas to Alaska, and on and on, yet infinitely different. This was not a journey of employment, cultural enlightenment, or even adventure (although doubtless it would have its share). It was a journey into my Self.

But I had no clue what it could look like. Jason's journey was not mine, of course, since I hate snakes, sweat and toilets without protective seat covers (much less without seats). So I waited, waited with active expectation while I eased into retirement, wrote every day, played with grandchildren, walked labyrinths ... lived my life and listened.

Then one morning as I stood at the window of our Manhattan apartment, sipping chai tea and gazing at the crisscrossing traffic on the Brooklyn Bridge, I heard it. A voice that sounded strangely like my own, but my mouth hadn't moved. I circled around to confirm that I had no unexpected company, then listened with heightened intensity.

"You love labyrinths. You love to write," the voice repeated. "Write about labyrinths ... one in every state."

The adrenaline rush pushed *Yes!* out of my mouth with the force of a champagne cork. "Yes!" I shouted. "This is it. This is my journey. I can do it!" From the first moment, I had no doubt—questions, but no doubt.

Surprisingly, within an hour I had sketched out the framework for the journey. I could access the locations, contact information and types of labyrinths from the online Worldwide Labyrinth Locator (www.labyrinthlocator.com). I would select outdoor labyrinths created by individuals in their own yards (or land they frequented), not professionally built nor commercially connected. The "built and/or envisioned by a woman" criteria would surface seven visits down the road when I noticed the pattern, a pattern I would follow faithfully for forty-three more states.

I needed to announce my idea to someone, to make it real in the world outside my own thoughts and walls of our apartment, so I called Marian, my friend of thirty years, in Connecticut. She was driving in a state where talking on the phone while driving is illegal; but she picked up anyway, just long enough to say, "Let me pull over." (We have some of our best conversations while she's sitting in her car in a parking lot.)

She listened to my gush of words, from idea to details, without interruption then said, "Twylla, this is wonderful! I love it. And I could go with you."

THIS BOOK IS a chronology of my journey across the United States to walk labyrinths and collect stories, beginning on Miramar Beach, Florida in May, 2012 and ending on Maui, Hawaii in July, 2014. It would have been decidedly easier to simply select labyrinths from the

World Wide Labyrinth Locator, walk them, then check them off my list and move on. But I knew that it was through the women's stories that I would realize my own.

I was taking a chance that the women I contacted, who knew nothing about me, would actually say yes to my email inquiry or phone call. They could have easily ignored an unknown name or number or politely refused my request. Of the fifty women I eventually visited, however, every one of them not only said yes, but a variation of "How exciting!" "I'm honored!" "Can you stay for lunch?"

I asked to stay an hour. Most places I left after two, three, even four.

Our common thread is a path—a peaceful, mindful walking path. A labyrinth. The women trusted, as did I, that our connections to the labyrinth would connect us to each other. It did and still does. Throughout the journey, I linked the women to one another via email and updates on my blog, "New York City Reflections." I passed one woman's story to the next and to the next. We are a community.

The final commonality is the four questions I asked each labyrinth creator:

1. What was your first labyrinth experience?
2. What prompted you to want to build your own labyrinth?
3. How did you build it?
4. What value does the labyrinth add to your life?

Their stories are grouped in chapters according to the trips I made, nineteen of them. I have attempted to capture the essence of each woman's story rather than provide a systematic rendering of answers to four questions. They tell their own stories in their own words. Experiences from my own journey are sprinkled throughout in journal entries and *En Route* reflections, moments to pull off the road and take in the view.

Whether you're on a journey of your own or pondering the possibilities; already connected to labyrinths or curious about them; a labyrinth builder or wanna-be builder; searching for a tool of meditation, stress reduction, spirituality; or like to hear a good story ...

Join us, all fifty-one of us, as we tell you ours.

1

Will This Really Work?

Florida

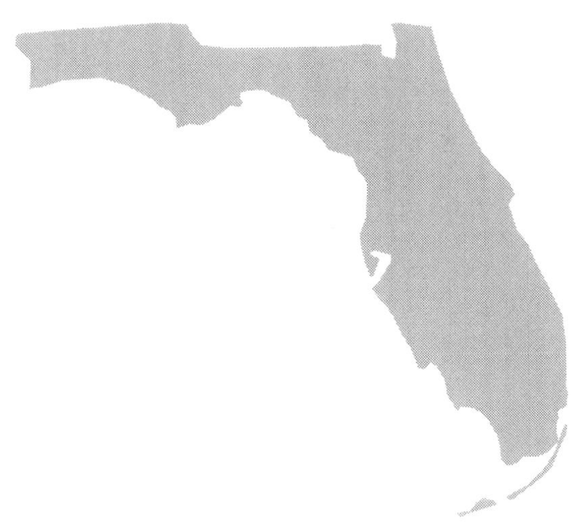

Anne Hornstein, Florida.

~ Twylla's journal ~

Grayton Beach, Florida
May 11, 2012

I DID IT! I made the call to a real person who built her own labyrinth. And she said YES!

Anne Hornstein and her labyrinth are only twenty minutes away. The nearest labyrinth to our vacation rental could be six hundred miles away in Miami rather than an easy drive down Highway 98 toward Destin. And Anne's description on the World Wide Labyrinth Locator sounds so inviting,

> "This sand labyrinth is available almost all year long, except when Grandmother Ocean comes up so high on the beach that she takes it away. Please come and enjoy this organic experience."

"How exciting!" she said when I explained my journey and that her labyrinth would be the first of fifty. "Would you like some company?"

Like some company? I didn't even have to ask if she would join me.

Tomorrow morning at 7:30. Meet at Pompano Joe's parking lot.

"I'll be riding a bicycle," Anne said.

How can I possibly go to sleep?

Anne Hornstein
Miramar Beach, Florida
May 12, 2012

SUGAR-WHITE SAND. Glittering turquoise water. Early morning beach walkers. I waved at the first and only woman cyclist that pedaled into the lot. She parked beside my car, hopped off and gave me a hug.

"The labyrinth is only about thirty yards down the beach. Let's leave our shoes here," Anne suggested.

"I built this labyrinth in January," she explained, sticking a feather's quill into the sand at its entrance. "It will usually last for several months unless we get a big tidal surge or the beach gets raked and fluffed. But then, I just build it back. One of the many metaphors I've learned from the labyrinth is the law of impermanence."

Anne and I knelt in the warm sand and fingered pieces of sand dollars, sticks, feathers and crispy brown sea grass outlining the labyrinth's path.

"It was right after 9/11 that I created my first beach labyrinth," she began reflectively. "I wanted to honor the people who had died, their families and friends left behind, and the support people involved. A friend of mine and I lined the labyrinth with sea grass and set votive candles around the perimeter. We placed a coffee can-size fire candle in the middle that you could see all along this stretch of beach. Others joined as we walked in prayer and reflection."

The waves' rhythmic back and forth held her gaze as she relived the moment.

"For ten days after that, I walked it every day as a meditation. Each time I walked, I learned more about the labyrinth, myself, and how we're all connected in this world.

"Let's walk it together!" Anne exclaimed, shifting moods as she clapped sand from her hands. "It's called tandem walking, just one of *1,000 Ways to Walk a Labyrinth*, a book I'm working on."

A thousand ways? I thought there was only one.

"Take my hand and we'll walk together as far as we can. I did this with kids once, and one of them said it was like we were dance partners," she laughed. We twirled under each other's arms at a turn, then parted, only to join hands moments later.

"I love how we can travel the same path, but do our own thing. Together and apart. Another labyrinth metaphor!" Anne sang as we twirled again.

Anne finished her walk a few minutes before I did and stretched out on the beach, her feet touching the waves as they pulsed in and out. She picked up on her story as I joined her.

"I've been walking labyrinths for about twenty-five years. My first was in Steamboat Springs, Colorado in the light of a full moon. It was so magical. I never imagined, then, that I would be building beach labyrinths in Florida.

"I left Colorado just to get out of town one winter about twenty years ago, headed to Shreveport, Louisiana on an extended road trip. The ocean started calling to me, so I decided to check out the Gulf of Mexico here in Destin. A few days turned into a few weeks then a few months, and I'm still living here—loving life! I wasn't even looking for a new place to live. I was just open to what was in front of me, and my life has continued to evolve."

Anne's voice became more animated as she described her life and passions. "I've become a Brain Gym consultant, a Matrix Energetics practitioner. I write. I facilitate labyrinth walks and teach others how to create them. I host Glad Hatter Tea Parties for children and help adults awaken their creative spirits. I call it Follow Your Heart Adventures. That's what we all want to do, isn't it? It's all about bringing the spirit of play and joy into people's lives.

"And I love to walk labyrinths, as you can tell. I usually walk this one every day, sometimes twice a day. I get inspired with new ideas, become centered and gain clarity about projects I'm working on. Every time I walk my labyrinth and select treasures from the beach to line the path, I'm planting seeds of love. I figure there's always room for more love."

At water's edge, I watched Anne pick up a stick and effortlessly draw a classical labyrinth in the sand. "I'll show you how," she smiled.

"You start with a cross, draw four dots" … and on and on she went, reciting directions as she drew. I squatted beside her, picked up my own stick, and in the smoothness of freshly washed sand, I drew my first labyrinth.

An hour into my journey, I knew I was on the right path.

2

Great Northeast Adventure, Part 1

Connecticut, Massachusetts, Vermont, New York

Top, left to right: Nancy Henderson, Connecticut; Sandy Cardinal, Massachusetts. Bottom, left to right: Hilary Cooper-Kenny, New York ; Karen Speerstra, Vermont.

~ Twylla's journal ~

On the train from Grand Central Station
to Waterbury, Connecticut
June 17, 2012

IT'S BEEN A month since I visited Anne in Florida. Her enthusiastic yes was the kick-start I needed. Now, I'm off! Four states in three days.

"Just call us Thelma and Louise," Marian said last night as we re-confirmed our rendezvous time. Not that either of us has ever seen the entire movie. Just snippets of a pair of women speeding down the highway in a convertible, hair flying in all directions, chasing adventure. Buckled securely in Marian's SUV — hair neatly coiffured, cruise control set precisely at the speed limit, organic snacks in the cooler — we'll bear little resemblance to the wilder duo, at least from the outside.

Nancy Henderson
Terryville, Connecticut
June 17, 2012

NANCY AND ROB didn't wait for our knock.

"Welcome, we're so honored you came!" Nancy said, reaching the car as I stepped onto the driveway. "I love sharing my labyrinth; it's in the backyard." Marian and I hurried to keep up as the couple led us around the garage and into air thick with the fragrance of freshly cut grass.

"This labyrinth is ten years old," Nancy explained as the four of us gathered at the entrance. "But it hasn't always looked this way. First it was moss, then sod. But there's too much shade, so we removed the grass and spread woodchips. I planted some low-lying vines to help define the path. I enjoy taking care of it like it's alive, which any outdoor labyrinth is.

Nancy's attentive care obviously extended beyond the labyrinth to manicured shrubs, flowerbeds and pots overflowing with scarlet and purple petunias.

"When I walk to the center," Nancy continued, "I pull weeds, rearrange woodchips and nurture moss and vines, whatever needs my attention. When I walk out, the labyrinth is fresher and brighter, and I find that my own path in the world has fewer obstacles."

She instinctively reached down and plucked a handful of stray weeds at her feet.

"My labyrinth is a classical seven-circuit based on the one at Wisdom House in Litchfield, about fifteen miles from here. It's the first one I walked.

"I attended a workshop there once," Marian said. "The grounds are so peaceful."

"That's what attracted me to it," Nancy agreed, "then I found the labyrinth. People were walking it so I just watched them for a while, then decided to try it out. From my first step, I felt calmer and more centered. Just before I reached the middle, a woman stepped into the labyrinth and I felt a rush of energy. It seemed to spiral ahead of her and flow through me like a gust of warm air. I knew then that I wanted to immerse myself in the labyrinth and share it with others, so I decided to build my own."

"Nancy came home and began reading books about labyrinths and did a lot of research on the internet about how to build them," Rob explained.

"I remember that we used a photo as a guide," Nancy added, "and worked our way out from the center, making adjustments for the turns and entrance. I decided on bricks, mingled with special rocks I had collected, to line the path."

She paused briefly and smiled. "Years before I built this labyrinth, though, I had a Fairy Circle. Would you like to see it? It's right there behind the trees."

"Fairy Circle?" I repeated, in a tone that hopefully sounded more interested than skeptical.

As soon as we crossed the line from sunshine to shade, decibels dropped to a hush and cool air refreshed. One of Rob's handcrafted metal sculptures—two black circles, one nestled within the other—stood half hidden among low-lying branches.

"I found this space years ago," Nancy began softly as we reached a circular clearing. "It felt alive and purposeful to me, with good vibes, like a vortex of energy. I nicknamed it the Fairy Circle. The paths that lead to it and back are similar to a labyrinth, but I wasn't aware of it at the time. Both places feel meditative, where I can release stress and sort out my worries, make plans and decisions."

A breeze rippled through leaves as we absorbed the stillness.

"Before you walk my labyrinth, I'd like to show you the center," Nancy said, guiding us back into sunlight. Marian and I joined her in a three-way circle around a gray stepping stone imprinted with a Celtic knot.

"Tokens are buried under this stone. They've been here since the night my friends and I dedicated the labyrinth. I asked them to bring a small token to add to the heart of the labyrinth, and when the time was right each woman entered carrying her token. The only thing I asked was that they remain silent and open to random thoughts. We circled to the center. I was last. One by one, we placed our tokens in a small hole I had dug, then I covered them with this stone. I made coin-sized clay pendants, embedded with a spiral symbol, and strung them on satin cords for each of my friends. We hung them around our necks then danced, sang and laughed all around the labyrinth. It was so joyful!"

I reached down, traced the Celtic knot with my fingertips and sensed the presence of women who had shared friendship around Nancy's labyrinth.

I felt like dancing.

* * *

Sandy Cardinal
Buckland, Massachusetts
June 18, 2012

Circles, really big circles, outlined with purple plants and tall grasses, filled the meadow where East Buckland and Hog Hollow roads intersected.

"Surely that's not the labyrinth," I commented to Marian as we turned off the road and up a hill. "It would be huge!"

Two people, Sandy and Glen, and two dogs (not formally introduced) crossed the front porch of the two-story log cabin to greet us.

"Hop on and I'll take you for a tour of our place before we visit the labyrinth," Sandy said as she settled behind the wheel of a golf cart. "Your visit is a welcome break from all the preparations for our Ninth Annual Lavender Festival next week."

Marian and I grasped anything nailed down as Sandy zipped down the hill toward The Conference Center (barn), zoomed back up to The Lavender Coop, then angled across the front yard to The Bird Sanctuary.

"I enjoy my life here on the hill," Sandy shared. "I was in personnel for thirty years and don't miss that life at all. There's so much on the land that keeps me busy, plus I've taken over the whole upstairs of our house where I weave, tat, and plan to learn how to use a spinning wheel. If people ask me what my life is like, I say variety and inconsistency."

We stood with our backs to the cooing doves and looked out over the meadow below. "Well, there it is! My labyrinth. You can see it from Google Earth—180 feet in diameter!"

"Wow!" I exclaimed, in a feeble attempt to express my amazement. Sandy flattened the accelerator to the floor and we sped toward the circles that Marian and I had spotted earlier from the road.

"Everyone wants to know, 'Why so big?' Well, when we bought the place in 2000, we had this open meadow and needed to use it for something. I considered grazing land, but realized that I didn't know anything about raising livestock and had little interest in learning. So the meadow waited for me for two years. Then I walked a neighbor's seven-circuit lavender labyrinth."

Sandy parked the cart beside a sign titled *The Labyrinth,* which highlighted basic information for walkers. One short sentence was set apart from the rest:

The goal is to enjoy - not to finish.

"I can't put words to the experience of walking that first labyrinth without ruining the impact it had on me," Sandy said, "but it brought me a clear understanding of what to do with this south-facing meadow.

"I PREFERRED THE eleven-circuit Chartres design," she continued, "with a path wide enough for two people to walk side-by-side or pass each other without needing to step off the path. I wanted to line it with lavender plants like my friend's, and they need about thirty-six inches of space when mature. Then, you just do the math. Eleven rings, with a four-foot-wide path, and three-foot-wide lavender border. The labyrinth quickly became an enormous 180 feet!"

Sandy brushed a bee from her face and laughed, "It was a comedy of errors to build. I first marked the concentric circles with wood ash, but they disappeared in the grass. Then I tried lime, thinking that if it works on football fields, it would work in the meadow; but the grass was too tall, and the lime disappeared too. My next attempt was earthy-friendly orange spray paint, but it turned into a huge smear after a week of rain. Finally, success! Blue Ford tractor paint stayed put."

"Smell the lavender?" she asked.

If purple possess a smell, it must be lavender. The air was rich with it.

"I began with 500 lavender plants twelve years ago, planted each one by hand, thinking they would fill up the labyrinth. They barely made a difference. I was so proud of them, though. I've added more over the years, plus perennials, ferns and grasses. You've come at a good time to walk it. You'll smell the lavender all the way around."

Sandy retrieved a white plastic bucket half full of weeds from the cart.

"I drag one of these five-gallon buckets behind me and weed for hours at a time. Some days I'll fill and empty twenty or more buckets. That's some of my best thinking time. I rarely walk it myself, but it gives me joy for others to walk it. I care for it. It's always changing."

Like its creator, I thought.

I took a deep breath of lavender and earth and strolled beside Marian on the wide path. Sandy would check on us when we reached the center ... in about an hour.

Karen Speerstra
Randolph Center, Vermont
June 18, 2012

Karen opened the front door. I noticed her warm smile first, then her purple hat, absent of hair beyond the narrow brim. I wondered. I had seen too many women of similar appearance over the years. I hoped I was mistaken.

"I could sit out here all day on a day like today," Karen sighed, pouring lemonade for Marian, me and her son, Joel, who joined us under the shade of an umbrella. "We found this place online. It was the only house we looked at in Vermont when we decided to move from Cambridge. The quiet. Oh, the quiet!"

"Did you notice the labyrinth," she asked, "on that sloping piece of ground before you get to the house? It can be a little hard to make out unless you know what you're looking for."

"We recognized the white marble that lines the path, just like you described on the World Wide Labyrinth Locator," I answered.

"That marble was quite the challenge!" she said, stretching out the last three words for emphasis. "I ordered two and a half tons and when it was delivered, the pieces were basketball rather than baseball size. My dear husband, John, chiseled them into manageable pieces.

"It's a Chartres design like the first one I walked at Grace Cathedral in San Francisco. What a thrill it was to step on that path. I saw the original at Chartres Cathedral years before, but couldn't walk it because it was covered with chairs, as is the case most of the time. I just knew I wanted one of my very own, and I thought it would be a great family project. Plus, I hoped that by building one, I might figure out how the creators of the Chartres labyrinth did it. That's always intrigued me."

Joel adjusted the umbrella while Karen passed the plate of cookies around.

"It's twelve years old now," she reflected. "Building it in 2000, for my sixtieth birthday present, was such a life-marker for me. When I walked it for the first time, I kept asking myself what this decade would bring. What was I supposed to do now that I was retired from the very hectic world of publishing? And the answer I got was, 'You have plenty of time.' So I planted thyme and flowers in the center and thyme along the edge.

"I was diagnosed with ovarian cancer three years later," she added quietly.

Slender leaves twirled silently on a metal tree sculpture a few yards away as Karen paused, momentarily, in her story. Marian, Joel and I observed the silence with her.

"Although I've been living with cancer for ten years now, I try not to let it define who I am. I think the labyrinth helped me accept what my body was up to. It's a calming, meditative tool—a constant in my life, like an old friend. Every time we drive up or down our driveway, I look at it and thank it. It will always be there when I come back."

* * *

SIX MONTHS AFTER Marian and I walked her labyrinth, Karen decided to suspend chemotherapy infusions and enter hospice care at home. She died on November 13, 2013.

Although we never again spoke personally, we emailed regularly. Karen was a few steps ahead of me on a path of discovery as a writer, as a woman on a spiritual and personal journey.

I was honored when she invited me to see her writing room before we left that day. Books overflowed from shelves onto the floor, perched on window ledges and any other flat surface they could find. Trees crowded around the window above her writing desk, like friends keeping watch through the night.

Karen showed me the books she had written and spoke of her latest research into the Divine Feminine. I remarked that I had first read about the Divine Feminine in Sue Monk Kidd's book *The Dance of the Dissident Daughter*, a life-changing book for me.

"It's one of my favorite books too! In fact, I quoted Sue in my book *Sophia, The Feminine Face of God: Nine Heart Paths to Healing and Abundance*." She pulled a copy from a shelf, retrieved a pen from her desk and signed the title page.

"I want you to have this," she smiled as she placed the book in my hands. "I think we're kindred spirits."

Karen accompanied us to the labyrinth, stepping carefully along the trail that led from her house. She sat on the weathered bench in the center where I took her picture. When I look at that photo today, I see a confident woman, comfortable with who she was—at that very moment—the only moment any of us ever has.

* * *

EN ROUTE

Castletown, VT
Bed and Breakfast
June 18, 2012

I WASN'T READY to be still tonight. Even after traveling all day, visiting with Sandy and Karen, I needed to keep moving. I left Marian curled up with a book on the sofa and drove the mile or so back into downtown Castleton, where earlier we had passed a market. Loaded down with fig newtons, peanut M&Ms and an apple, I made a U-turn and headed back.

As I passed the library, I noticed the door was open. The red brick building looked like something straight out of colonial America, with matching chimneys on each end and a white cupola on the roof. I felt a strong urge to enter but thought, "Why? I don't need to visit a library tonight."

I drove by, braked after five seconds, reversed, and parked near the sidewalk leading to the front door. Something told me I needed to be in that library.

"Can I help you find something?" a young woman asked as I walked in.

"No thanks, I just want to look around." Then on second thought added, "Do you happen to have any brochures about the history of this building?"

"I don't, but my mother could probably help you. She's the librarian."

About that time, Jan, the mother-librarian, approached and introduced herself.

"It's nice to meet you," I replied. "I'm Twylla. Do you have anything I could read about this building?"

Jan stared at me. "What did you say your name was?" she asked.

"Twylla."

She continued staring then said, "My daughter's name is Twylla." She waved her Twyla (with one L, I later discovered) over from the desk by the front door.

"Twyla, meet Twylla," Jan said to her daughter.

For the first time in my life, I stood face-to-face with another Twylla. Chill bumps raced up my arms and legs, dropping my body temperature by the second. With tears in my eyes, I instinctively embraced Twyla, a young woman I had never met but who shared something that no one in my life ever had.

"You're the first person I've ever met with my name," she said.

"Me, too, but it's taken me a few years longer than you," I laughed.

Jan turned to me and asked, "Do you know what your name means?"

I shrugged. "No, not really. My mother told me that she named me after a doll she had when she was a little girl. She never knew where the name came from."

"When our Twyla was born, we searched and searched for just the right name. The origin of Twyla/Twylla is *twil,* from an old English word for 'woven of two threads' that symbolizes strength."

Twylla.

Woven of two threads. Strong.

The woman I want to be.

The woman, my name tells me, I already am.

Hilary Cooper-Kenny
Hudson Falls, New York
June 19, 2012

Crazy as a Loom Weaving Studio, a house built in 1790, and a seven-circuit labyrinth in the backyard ... all seemingly unconnected pieces. Yet one woman ties them masterfully together.

"Do you want to see the labyrinth first or come in and look around the weaving studio?" Hilary asked, shortly after we knocked on the screened door.

My mouth was on its way to forming an answer when she continued.

"Oh, come on in first and I'll show you around. Things are in a bit of a jumble because I'm getting ready for a weaving weekend and apprenticing Lois here."

Marian and I uttered a quick, "Hi, nice to meet you," to Lois as Hilary led us into the first of several high-ceilinged rooms. Each space was filled with a feast of color—stacks of fabric, spools of thread, rugs, hats, seat cushions, dishtowels, blankets—everything woven or soon to be woven.

"This house was listed for sale six years ago," Hilary began in the foyer. "I actually drove by it every day on my way to work, but all I could clearly see was the eyebrow window over the front door. It was so overgrown, taken over by bushes and vines. As soon as I walked in the door, though, I knew I had to have it for my looms. I could see myself weaving here. It made my heart sing.

"My husband and I already had a couple of mortgages," she continued on our way up the stairs, "and he didn't share my vision for this place. I told him, 'You don't have to like what I like,' and I bought it on my own. You have to have faith. After eight months of renovation, I moved my looms in and have been weaving and teaching others to weave ever since."

Words of encouragement appeared on wooden signs in every

room: IMAGINE, DREAM, KEEP IT SIMPLE. A Thoreau quote flowed across a white board:

> "If one advances confidently in the direction of his dreams and endeavors to live the life he has imagined, he will meet with a success unexpected in common hours."

"SOME OF MY students are intimidated when they see a loom for the first time," Hilary said pausing beside an intricate wooden version, roughly the size of Marian's car. "But I tell them to concentrate only on what they're doing at the moment. I ask them, 'Can you do this step?' Once they say yes, I tell them that's all they need to think about. Kind of like walking a labyrinth, don't you think? And it's about time we went to see it."

Matching Hilary's pace, we were half way to the labyrinth before the screened door slammed behind us. She strode directly to the center and stood beside a three-tiered fountain.

"I built the labyrinth here because this is where it belongs. I considered another part of the yard, but I didn't feel it anywhere else. The area was grown up with knotweed so it needed some clearing, but I didn't cut down any trees. I wanted a special and serene place here at the studio. I'm a Type-A personality, really driven. It pulls me back and centers me.

"Before I built it," she explained, "I practiced drawing it over and over until I could draw it without thinking about it. Then I came out here and marked it with spray paint. Be sure and wear a mask if you ever do that!

"And these pebbles," she said, rearranging rocks with the toe of her shoe, "are my second attempt at covering the path. I initially planted grass, but decided that battling weeds interfered with the peacefulness of the place. I wanted the labyrinth to express my connection to all that is good, calm and uncomplicated."

"What made you build it in the first place?" Marian asked.

"It's because of my grandson," Hilary smiled. "I took him and his older brother, ages eight and eleven at the time, to my friend's nature sanctuary. She had a labyrinth, and we all walked it. The older one kept saying, 'I don't get it;' but the younger one said, 'I think I know with it means. It's where you find the center of your heart.' When he said that, I just had to come home and build one."

Hilary returned to the studio to continue her preparations. Marian tagged along to take a second look at a purple hat that had caught her eye. I wove my way along the curving path—back, forth, around and round—to the center of my heart.

3

Great Northeast Adventure, Part 2

Rhode Island, New Hampshire, Maine

Top, left to right: Linda Phelan, Rhode Island; Donna Mcgowen, Maine. Bottom: Lyrion Ap Tower, New Hampshire.

~ Twylla's journal ~

On the train from Grand Central Station
to Waterbury, Connecticut
August 29, 2012

I ALMOST DIDN'T contact Linda in Rhode Island. Like Hilary's Crazy as a Loom Weaving Studio in New York, the title—The Healing Co-Operative Women's Cancer Resource Center—sounded like a business. But Linda assured me, as did Hilary, that her labyrinth story is very personal.

New Hampshire is next, where Marian and I will meet our first High Priestess of a pagan community, Lyrion, who describes herself as a witch.

Then on to visit Donna in Brunswick, Maine. The last, and only, time I visited Maine was when Drew, Katherine [daughter] and I, joined Jason [son] on the Appalachian Trail for two days. He was relatively close to the beginning of his journey, as am I. But he was a lot ... dirtier.

Linda Phelan
Middletown, Rhode Island
August 29, 2012

"THE LABYRINTH'S ACROSS the driveway surrounded by those spiky shrubs," Linda said, as she poked her head out the front door of the Healing Co-op's office. "I'll join you shortly." Ten minutes later, she, Marian and I sat on a grassy slope above the labyrinth, shoeless.

"My sister, Mary, who happens to be an amazing artist and equally as crazy as I am, spray-painted this labyrinth with me on a very cold and very wet October weekend ten years ago," Linda laughed. "We covered the entire eighty feet with sod, on our hands and knees.

I walk it barefoot whenever I can. I need to feel the earth under my feet.

"I named it Veriditas, which means the greening power of the earth. Are you familiar with Hildegard of Bingen?" she asked. "She used the term often in her writing."

"I learned of her only last month," I answered, "in a book by Karen Speerstra, the woman whose labyrinth I visited in Vermont. Hildegard was a Benedictine abbess, right?"

"Yes, in Germany. In the twelfth century, she wrote so insightfully that everything on earth is connected.

"It was actually in Germany that I walked my first labyrinth with my German grandmother," she went on. "I was a little girl and all I remember is that the labyrinth was made of stones. But I connected to it, even as a child. Throughout my life, I've been drawn to find labyrinths, to walk and pray in them. Then when I founded the Healing Co-op, I wanted to build one as a symbolic representation of what we could create on this property for the cancer population."

She leaned back and dug her toes into the warm grass. "The shrubs that line the path are all yew. We chose yew because the chemotherapy drug, Toxol, is derived from it. They were planted, one-

by-one, by the women of the Healing Co-op and me.

"Why a cancer center for women, in particular?" Marian said.

"I've been on my own journey with cancer for over twenty years," Linda replied. "I was diagnosed with it twenty-two years ago and told I had three years to live. My mother and maternal aunt died of breast cancer. My vision for this center lived deep in my heart before it evolved into what you see today.

"This Healing Co-op is a place where women with all types of cancer, and their families and friends, can find support while making the healing journey toward life, or death."

Linda stood and stepped toward the wooden arbor at the labyrinth's entrance. "The labyrinth is our centering place. Before and after our support groups, the women (who can) walk it. And we walk it when one of our members dies, in gratitude for her life, for knowing her. It's an opportunity for change for some, acceptance for others, for people to be whoever they are. It's about self-love.

"Plus it's always open to the public," she added. "We have senior citizen groups, individuals with disabilities, children with autism, anyone, come walk it."

A car drove up and parked in front of the office. Linda returned a woman's wave.

"I wish I could join you, but I have an appointment. I walked the labyrinth early this morning, which I usually do every day, either then or at dusk. It feels like an anchor; it calms my spinning mind. Have a peaceful walk."

Marian sat on one of the concrete benches in the center while I circled. Later, we shared our thoughts. Not surprisingly, they were the same—thoughts of women we knew whose lives had been affected by cancer. Shannon, Jan, Kathleen, Chris, Debbie, Bonnie, Karen ... and now Linda.

* * *

On August 4, 2014, two years after our visit, I received an email from Linda:

> "During the construction of a new home on the property, we were told by the Department of Environmental Management that we are in violation having the labyrinth too close to wetlands. I have owned this property for twenty-five years, and in no way does the labyrinth threaten wetlands or anything of its kind. Nevertheless, we are being made to deconstruct it. I am devastated, to say the least. It has created so much stress, tears, and upset in my heart and spirit. I have to let it go. I have transplanted sixty yew and hope that people will come this week to take a shrub or two before they have to be mowed down."

In my memory, Linda's labyrinth remains, lined with yew, tending to all who enter. The land has been made forever sacred by the footsteps of those who walked it and by the love of the woman who created it.

Lyrion Ap Tower
Wilton, New Hampshire
August 30, 2012

A black-faced cat, with matching paws and sleek brown body, darted in front of the car as Marian parked in the driveway. Clearly on a mission, it leaped onto a shaded granite bench seconds later, stretched and lay down. The bench, we noticed, was in the center of a spiral.

"Come on in the kitchen and join me for a cup of homemade tea," Lyrion called from the steps at the side of the house. The door opened and we were mesmerized.

Bunches of dried plants hung upside down from beams; stems and leaves floated in liquid-filled jars; vegetation, in an array of forest greens and crispy browns, covered the counters. Scents from pungent to perfumed filled our noses with question marks.

"You'll see from my collection that I love plants," Lyrion smiled. "I'm an herbalist.

"I'm constantly learning about the healing properties of plants and making brews," she said. "My husband, Raven, and I lead Wildcrafting walks to teach people how to locate, harvest, and safely prepare native herbs. I hope he'll be home before you leave. He's the botanist and can tell you more about our place, which is a Certified Wildlife Habitat. Bring your tea and let's look at the labyrinth."

Stepping between two gray granite posts, Lyrion began, "We chose the spiral because it holds a great deal of significance to us. As Pagans and Witches, Nature is our temple. Raven and I wanted a deliberately quiet, cathedral-like space among the trees, available to all faiths. I had seen labyrinths and spirals in gardening and photography books and on a deck of spiritual garden cards. I was enchanted and knew right away that we had to create one."

Neither Marian nor I had ever met a Pagan, Witch, or herbalist. We stood in the center of a spiral with a woman who was all three. We did the only thing that felt respectful. We listened.

"The spiral is one of the oldest and most widespread spiritual symbols," Lyrion explained. "It represents the cyclic nature of life's path—birth, growth, adulthood, aging, death and rebirth. The Pagan/Wiccan concept of a lifetime is more spiral than linear. We don't believe we're merely born, live and die. Witches come around each year to the same dates as before; but in growing older, we gain knowledge, experience, love and wisdom in the passage.

"The direction you walk is symbolic too," she went on, circling her hand first to the left then the right. "You enter counterclockwise, or moon wise, and let go of worldly cares. Sit peacefully in the center; then exit clockwise, or sun wise. Take whatever peace, understanding or answers you gained. It's like journeying to the center of the Self."

The cat yawned and repositioned herself on the sunnier corner of the bench.

I dream in the spiral," Lyrion smiled, "and talk to the goddess a lot. As High Priestess of this community, it's my job to serve, to make sure that those who don't have basic needs, like food and clothing, get them. I walk out with intention. It puts my feet on the right path."

A car pulled into the driveway. Raven stepped out and we shook hands.

"You're just in time to tell them about how we built the labyrinth," Lyrion said.

"Well, the short version," Raven began, "is that we started with the math—how much space we had for the center, surrounding trees and path. Then Lyrion stood in the center with one end of a rope attached to her staff and the other wrapped around a bucket filled with cornmeal. I scribed the spiral path by unwinding the rope as I walked around the center, leaving a line of cornmeal. We put the word out to our Pagan community to bring river stones to place on that line. The response was overwhelming."

"So the labyrinth is a part of your Certified Wildlife Habitat?" I asked.

"Our entire five acres is a safe home for wildlife, a year-round source of food, water and shelter. The land is a spiritual place as well as a teaching environment," Raven clarified, leading us across the backyard to stand beneath a large white pine.

"This tree is named Theophilia, Beloved of God. It's a gathering place for our community," Lyrion shared. "Some of them are coming tomorrow night for our Blue Moon Gathering. We'll walk the labyrinth, and you're welcome to join us."

I explained that we had an appointment in Brunswick that afternoon but would like to walk the labyrinth before we left. As we stepped onto the moss-covered path a few minutes later, we noted that we were not alone. The bench was still occupied.

* * *

Donna Mcgowen
Brunswick, Maine
August 30, 2012

In preparing to write Donna's chapter, I opened a Ziploc bag, which had been sealed for two and a half years. A slip of paper, in my hurried handwriting, escaped:

Grass from Maine Labyrinth

I eagerly anticipated the fragrance that had captivated me the day of our visit. I took a deep breath. Nothing. I was disappointed but not surprised. I knew the chances were slim that the sweetness would have lasted beyond that day, but I had to try. I had to try to capture the single-most powerful memory I carried with me from that afternoon.

"The labyrinth's beyond those two footbridges," Donna pointed out, as Marian and I followed her down a gentle slope past the house.

Emerald green grassland, roughly the size of a soccer field, spread out below, edged with wildflowers and grasses that had survived the mower's grasp. Without warning, I caught my first whiff of unidentified sweetness.

"I grew up here, left, then moved back twelve years ago when my mother died," Donna said while the three of us settled into Adirondack chairs a few feet from the labyrinth. "When I returned, I knew that I had to have a labyrinth here. This land has seen much violence in the past with Indian wars. The labyrinth is part of the healing that's happening, along with vision quests, drumming, sweat lodges, meditation and energy work.

"I believe that the land picks you," she went on. "You're led to where you need to be. This space is my responsibility.

"My friend, David Anthony Curtis, walked the meadow with me and we both asked Spirit to show us the perfect place for the labyrinth. We were led to this spot. A seven-circuit labyrinth fit perfectly. Once I had collected enough stones to line the path, I asked a couple of other friends to join David and me in building it. We finished it in one afternoon, if you can believe that. It was a lot of work!"

Donna glanced over her shoulder toward the labyrinth and continued, "David's labyrinth in Phippsburg, Maine was the first one I walked. He facilitated walks every Sunday afternoon, and I went with a friend. The ceremony was very honoring. It brought me into myself and into the present moment. It was like a walking meditation. I knew that I was in a special place."

My gaze followed hers to the labyrinth's center where a gray, dead or dying tree stood. Its remaining three limbs were frozen in a half twist.

"Tell me about that tree," I said, thinking that it seemed out of place in the midst of a vibrant labyrinth.

"It was an apple tree, over a hundred years old. All trees have their life span, but it's sad to see a member of my family pass. Maybe it took on some of the intense energy that this area has experienced. It sustains other life now, though. Birds perch on its limbs, along with my rescue cat, Mae Mae.

"Why don't you two go ahead and walk it, and I'll catch up with you when you're finished?" Donna suggested. "I need to check on a couple of house guests. I weed-whacked the path yesterday so it will be easier to walk."

I paused momentarily at the entrance for late afternoon sun to warm my face, then stepped past an angel poised in prayer. A rush of the illusive fragrance grabbed my nose. It pulled me along the path like a cartoon character lured by the swirling aroma of an apple pie cooling on a windowsill. I leaned against the tree into quietness, punctuated only by crickets' chatter, mindlessly fingering grass clippings. The sweet smell instantly magnified. I stuffed both pockets full and remained with eyes closed until Marian alerted me that Donna was waiting.

She met us at the second footbridge. "What did you think?"

"Such peace," I answered simply.

"I'm so glad you felt it. I walk every day. It gives me peace of mind and a place to say prayers. I stand in the middle and send light and peace to the land, the world and the universe. I enter with an open mind, with intention to give and receive. If I have a question, I ask it. By the time I finish, I have the answer."

I pulled a pinch of grass clippings from my pocket. "The labyrinth is alive with this fragrance. Is there a name for it?"

"I'm not sure, but I don't think it's any one type of grass," Donna answered. "More a mixture of grasses, plus clover and wildflowers. Cutting it yesterday must have set the fragrance free."

Two days later, I emailed Donna to thank her for the visit. It was only then that I noted her user name—meadowsweetdonna. Of course.

4

Labyrinths and Battlefield

New Jersey, Pennsylvania, Maryland

Top, left to right: Bianca Franchi, New Jersey; Marty Jones, Pennsylvania. Bottom: Kathleen Rosemary and Susan Gardener, Maryland.

~ Twylla's journal ~

October 22, 2012
Manhattan apartment

I JUST GOT off the phone with Bianca.

"I know you're scheduled to visit in a couple of days, but you may not want to come," she said. "I have to be totally honest. My labyrinth is in a state of disrepair, and you probably won't even be able to walk it."

My heart sank. Bianca's labyrinth is in a perfect location, just an hour from the White Plains train station where Marian is picking me up. It meets all the criteria: outdoors, built by a woman, no commercial connection. I don't want to begin a new search.

And why should I?

Listening to Bianca's voice, I knew this was a woman I wanted to meet. Does it matter that I won't be able to walk her labyrinth?

"Bianca, does your labyrinth have a story to tell?" I asked.

She answered immediately, "Absolutely, and I'd love to share it with you!"

That was all I needed to know.

"I can't wait to hear it and meet you," I told her.

I imagined that her smile matched mine.

Bianca Franchi
Denville, New Jersey
October 24, 2012

BIANCA, OR WHO we assumed was Bianca, flagged us down as we scanned mailboxes for #233. "You must be the labyrinth ladies!" she said. (How could she possibly know?) "I was just finishing my walk. Follow me." She ushered us into the driveway, then pointed across the road. "The labyrinth's over there."

"I told you on the phone that my labyrinth's in a state of disrepair, and now you can see for yourself," Bianca said," handing us an umbrella to share. "I just didn't want you to expect a pristine labyrinth. Like I said, I don't think there's any way you can walk it."

Disrepair felt like a tame word for the destruction that lay at our feet. I scoured the area for any landmark of the labyrinth's presence, but found only one curved string of ten or twelve rocks that bore any resemblance to the pattern. Nothing more.

"What caused this?" I asked.

"Hurricane Irene," Bianca answered, staring straight ahead, as if still in shock. "It uprooted the tree in the center and jumbled all the rocks along the path, even the landscape fabric underneath. I called it my Hug-A-Tree labyrinth because I loved to hug the tree when I got to the center. Now, there's just that stump left. The top of the tree landed on my roof behind you.

"I've been so busy repairing the house that I haven't gotten around to the labyrinth; but ever since I got your email, I've been thinking about renewing it," she said, a faint smile returning to her face. "Let's get out of this drizzle. There's a friend in my house I want you to meet.

"Marian and Twylla, meet Carol House. She's the one who introduced me to labyrinths and helped me build mine in 2008."

Bianca bustled between kitchen and dining table, tempting us with one homemade dish after another, like we were family she was trying to fatten up. Blueberry muffins with tea, then vegetable soup followed by scrambled eggs, toast and cranberry jam.

"She's Italian," Carol explained.

"I met Carol in Morristown, New Jersey at the Unitarian Fellowship Center," Bianca said, pouring tea. "She was presenting a program on labyrinths and brought a portable canvas one. That's the first one I ever walked. When I decided to build my own, Carol helped me lay out the seven circuits."

"I've been walking labyrinths for over twenty years," Carol said.

"I have three on my property in Blairstown, New Jersey. I was happy to help Bianca build hers. She had already selected the location for her labyrinth, and I used my dowsing rods to ask the earth where to place the entrance."

"Right out there, on that curve in the road," Bianca pointed. "That's where I wanted it. People pass that spot all the time as they walk the road that circles the lake. I've named that road the Sacred Loop because it has such energy from the generations who have lived here before us, especially Native Americans. A labyrinth would be a natural way to bring people together and provide something of significance to the community.

"More toast?" she asked.

"I started building the house first, but the labyrinth just wouldn't keep quiet. It came to be this annoying voice that I had to listen to, so I stopped work on the house and built the labyrinth. Since then I've learned that you need to honor that voice, the one that tells you to interrupt, or even change, the plan you think you're supposed to follow."

I let those words settle, making a note on my yellow legal pad to revisit their wisdom.

"I wish you could have seen my labyrinth before the hurricane," Bianca added, more softly. "I planted a red maple, pine, lilac, bleeding heart and some creeping myrtle beside the ancestor trees that surrounded it."

"You must miss having it in your life," I said.

"I do, but I'm trying not to be too invested in the past. When I step back and look at the labyrinth's disrepair, I realize it's like starting over, like a different stage of life. I'm trying to honor the process. It's become a form of gratitude for me, a reminder to take what you're dealt and celebrate the life within. It's my light shining."

Two days later, I received a voice mail from Bianca.

"I just wanted you to know that after you and Marian left, I called some workers to move out the heavy pieces, then I renewed the labyrinth. Your visit inspired me. I renamed it the "Sticks and Stones Labyrinth" because I replaced much of the wood with stone so it would be stronger. Come back and walk it anytime!"

Marty Jones
Mechanicsburg, Pennsylvania
October 24, 2012

"My sister, Marty, has a labyrinth too," Sandy mentioned as we were leaving her Massachusetts labyrinth in June."When you go to Pennsylvania, you should visit hers. Four months later, Marian and I were sipping homemade apple cider on Marty's screened-in porch.

"Sandy told me all about your visit," Marty said. I wonder if we'll be the only sisters with labyrinths that you meet on your journey—surely, the only sisters with lavender labyrinths. That's what I named mine, Lavender Labyrinth. I just like saying it!"

"So do we," I laughed. "I challenged Marian to a Lavender Labyrinth Tongue Twister contest on the drive here. Three times fast! We're still working on it."

"Sandy gave me bunches of lavender when we built my labyrinth. I had this section of land beside the house with nothing on it, so I decided to create my own. I called her to ask how to do it but realized that what I really needed was Sandy herself. So she came.

"It was a misty Wednesday morning in the spring of 2005," Marty recalled. "We started with a cup of tea, then changed our clothes and got to work. We dug up the ground with tillers, peeled up the sod and laid out the classic seven-circuit design. By Friday at supper, we were all done."

Marty refilled our glasses with sparkling amber cider from their orchard as she continued. "I'm kind of like Sandy in that tending the labyrinth is what I like to do best. I rarely walk it. Some days I think that I'll go sit in the center in the sunshine but usually don't find the time. I feel good when I'm out there working in it.

"Bring your cider with you," Marty said. "You need to see the labyrinth while the sun's still shining on it. The maple tree in the path is pretty spectacular this time of year."

Spectacular was the perfect word, although magnificent would have been an equally worthy superlative. A double ball of yellow—sun behind golden leaves—dazzled against a cobalt blue sky. The labyrinth mirrored the glow, with a carpet of newly fallen leaves cushioning the path.

"My husband Steve bought three maples at a public sale many years ago and thought they were all sugar maples, but it turned out that this one isn't. It was a bit of a challenge to fit the path around it when we built the labyrinth.

"But solving problems is, actually, something I like to do," Marty explained, "like finding plants tall and straight enough to line the path without drooping over and interfering with the walk. And figuring out how to put in edging so weeding isn't an overwhelming chore is an on-going challenge. Steve and I finally solved the mowing problem when we found a lawnmower that perfectly mows the eighteen-to-nineteen inch path.

"And this summer's project," she smiled, running her hand over clusters of dried stems, "is serious thinning of the Siberian Iris. They've done a little too well in the labyrinth."

A few rows over, Marian bent over what appeared to be a single file of chickens. "You have so many whimsical items all around the labyrinth," she remarked. "I love the cat over there, gazing up at the base of the birdhouse, and that metal dog looking this way. I swear he's about to run over here and lick me."

"Thanks!" Marty laughed. "I like finding things that feel right for a spot. At one time I had a whole set of brightly painted birdhouses on posts spread around the labyrinth, but most have rotted by now. Steve gave me a granite owl for Christmas, and I'm still trying to decide where to place it."

Marty knelt beside a terra cotta brick with the word LIFE printed on it.

"You'll probably recognize these bricks like the ones in Sandy's labyrinth. She made all of them. Right from the start, I knew I wanted her to create the seven synonyms for God that we work with in Christian Science. You'll find TRUTH, LOVE, SPIRIT, SOUL, PRINCIPLE and MIND scattered around the labyrinth," Marty explained. "Sometimes I'll pick one concept to consider as I weed a particular row, like PRINCIPLE. It means order, so I might focus on that in an area that seems out of control in some way.

"And these, of course." She moved a few feet further along the path where two side-by-side bricks spelled LAVENDER LABYRINTH."

Two sisters. Two lavender labyrinths.

Each labyrinth is a unique reflection of the woman who cares for it season after season, who infuses it with parts of herself.

EN ROUTE

Gettysburg National Military Park
October 25, 2012

GETTYSBURG. A PLACE I've wanted to visit for as long as I can remember, and this side trip wasn't even my idea. It was Marian's.

"Let's take a day and go to Gettysburg," she suggested. "It's only about forty-five minutes from Marty's house. I know how much you like Civil War stuff."

A good friend pays attention.

AT THE VISITOR Center, I read familiar facts:

- Three-day battle, July 1–3, 1863.
- Largest of the Civil War—85,000 Union troops, 75,000 Confederate.
- Costliest—51,000 soldiers killed, wounded or missing, about the same number on both sides.

- Turning point; Union victory from which the South did not recover.

The guide on the bus tour heaped more facts on these basics as we passed by scenes of battle: Cemetery Ridge, The Wheatfield, Peach Orchard, Devil's Den. I began to feel claustrophobic—too many numbers, too many names, too much information. I needed to escape the bus and breathe, to listen to the land.

At Little Round Top, I had my chance. While the guide and his entourage walked the rocky summit, I sat cross-legged on a flat, gray boulder and looked at the valley below. Browning grassland stretched from the base of the hill to lines of orange-tinted trees in the distance. Clumps of black-eyed Susans filled in gaps between rocks. Feathery, purple-tipped grasses swayed as breezes passed. Birds chirped. I turned around to locate them but instead met the gaze of a glossy, black artillery gun ... pointed directly at my head.

Union troops held the hill as Confederate soldiers scrambled up its face on the second day of battle. I felt their presence, heard their screams, their boots scraping against rock, smelled gunpowder mixed with sweat and the stench of their ruined flesh. I opened my clinched eyes. The land, only, remained.

Land that had witnessed staggering violence, unbearable pain, anger, hatred, sadness. Land that had soaked up the blood of thousands and absorbed bodies, one hole at a time.

Land that now lay peacefully before me—healed—one season after the next, after the next.

My mind could never comprehend the violence, never accept that war solved differences, never fathom the depth of grief for loved ones lost.

All I could do was sit and rest, among the sacred.

Susan Gardener and Kathleen Rosemary
Baltimore, Maryland
October 26, 2012

MARIAN PARKED IN front of a two-story red brick with a pumpkin perched on the top step. Traffic sped by in both directions. A horn honked. A boy waved from his bike. A woman pushed a stroller. Marian and I stepped directly from the sidewalk onto a labyrinth, which filled the entire front yard.

"So, how do you like our urban labyrinth?" Susan asked, once the four of us were comfortably settled in the living room with cups of tea and pumpkin bread.

"Amazing! I would have never thought of transforming a front yard into a labyrinth," I answered.

"From the street I thought it was a flower garden," Marian added. "Then when we got up close, I saw the design; but it's an octagon. I didn't know that labyrinths could be any other shape except round."

"Oh sure they can," Rose explained. "I researched octagons of different sizes for our space, took the measurements, then fit that design into it. It's about 25 x 25. It turned out to be quite the process, about a year and a half. We had to cut down a tree, take out the roots, use a sod cutter to remove the grass, then level the ground. I used square pavers, so I had to cut them to make bends and turns."

"Our vision all along was to incorporate gardens into it," Susan continued. "We started out with thyme, lavender, and rosemary, then added flowering plants and more herbs over the last three years. I'm excited that so many of them are still in full bloom, even our late-blooming roses."

"Talk about visions, it was Susan's to build a labyrinth in the first place." Rose smiled as she nodded in Susan's direction.

"I've definitely been aware of them for at least thirty years," Susan said, reaching for her cup of tea cooling on the table. "But it wasn't until I walked one at The Peace Conference thirteen years ago that

I was inspired to have my own. I came home knowing that somewhere, someday, a labyrinth would be part of my living space."

"And Susan, don't you remember when you introduced me to the labyrinth? It was at a friend's house who had created a small labyrinth out of stones in her front yard. I fell in love with the experience. That's where we got the idea to build one in our own yard."

"What's it like for your whole front yard to be a labyrinth?" I asked. "It's very public."

Susan sat forward on the edge of her chair. "Exactly!" she said with obvious excitement. "Our labyrinth has developed community, being just a step off the sidewalk. It's become a centering point. We meet our neighbors as they stop and ask questions about it. Young boys on their bikes stop and look. Sometimes they drop their bikes and jump across the pavers, even run it."

"We plan to erect a peace pole beside the labyrinth, right over there," Rose said, pointing out the window. "It will be another way to share the message of peace and understanding."

"A Peace Pole?" Marian asked.

"Yes, it's an actual pole," Rose clarified, "with the words *May Peace Prevail on Earth* in the language of the country it's located in, plus different languages on the other sides."

"Come on, let's go walk!" Susan declared, with the enthusiasm of an aerobics instructor.

A group walk made sense, on a labyrinth that clearly embraced Susan and Rose's commitment to community. Our community of four talked, laughed and stopped to finger a flower or admire treasures along the path—the bust of St. Francis cradling a lamb or a slightly rusted crescent moon with a star dangling from its pointy tip.

"I walk the labyrinth in times of struggle," Rose offered. "I walk, then I can let 'it' go, whatever 'it' is. Sometimes I try to control situations. The labyrinth helps me be patient, be who I am, and do what I can do."

Susan stopped as we reached the center. "I experience something different every time I walk. I ask a question and allow the answer to come. Our labyrinth is a sanctuary, a sacred, non-political area, a place of quiet. And it's dedicated to all the women in our families who came before us."

On a busy Baltimore street, Marian and I had discovered a place of contemplation and peace. I visualized the peace pole standing erect beside the labyrinth, together welcoming all who passed, inviting them to stop and breathe.

SUSAN AND ROSE installed their peace pole on September 21, 2014—International Day of Peace. *May Peace Prevail on Earth* is written around it in eight languages.

5

Traveling Solo, Except for Michael J. Fox

Oklahoma

Sharon Owen, Oklahoma.

~ Twylla's journal ~

Greenbrier, Arkansas home
November 30, 2012

I'M LEAVING TOMORROW morning to drive to Muskogee. I picked Sharon's labyrinth in Oklahoma because of distance—a three-and-a-half hour drive from our Arkansas home—and Sharon's kind reply to my email, "You are most welcome to come walk the labyrinths (two) and visit."

I'll miss Marian; but as grateful as I am for her company, I need to travel parts of this path alone. From the beginning, I wanted a journey that would test me, stretch me, even make me wonder, "Can I do this?" A journey where I would be the only one to make a decision, the only one to ask, "So, what do you think?" ... and the only one to listen to the sound of my own voice, growing stronger.

Truth be told, I'm not *totally* alone. Michael J. Fox agreed to tag along and read from his book, *Always Looking Up: The Adventures of an Incurable Optimist.* I forgot to ask if he'd ever been to Oklahoma.

Sharon Owen
Muskogee, Oklahoma
December 1, 2012

I SWITCHED OFF Michael in mid-sentence as I spotted Sharon eagerly waving from a chair at the end of her driveway. I recognized the scene from her email: large front yard, pecan trees, black table and chairs, fire pit. Mounds of white ash smoldered in the brick-lined pit, its warmth no longer needed on an unusually warm December day.

From a cooler at her feet, Sharon offered me a bottled water. "As you relax after that drive, I'll give you some background so you'll better understand my labyrinths," she offered.

"My great-great grandmother was Cherokee. She made medicines from plants and wrote them down in a book, which unfortunately has been lost. I've taught myself about the healing properties of herbs. Each plant has its own energetics and nature spirits and *devas.*"

"Elemental friends, like tree spirits," she continued, "show themselves and help us work with nature in co-creation. When we are open to trees, flowers, a creek or clouds, we encounter an actual wisdom, one that is not separate from our own but part of a collective consciousness."

SHARON PICKED UP a bundle of bird feathers, bound together by a strip of rawhide. "My feather smudge wand," she explained. "A Choctaw friend gifted it to me. I use it to disperse the smoke of white sage—for cleansing—followed by sweet grass, which protects and invites in the good." She demonstrated as I breathed deeply of imagined smoke circling our heads.

"Let's walk over to my smaller labyrinth," she said, leading me to the far side of the house. "I call it Well Laby because it's built beside the well and water flows underneath. As I walked the property in 1998, this area had a different feel to me, like a bubble dome of energy. The nature spirits told me that it is a sacred area, so I thought, 'This would be a good place for a labyrinth.' I asked the spirits first, and they gave me a big okay.

"I spray painted a seven-circuit design on the grass," she continued, "then one of my daughter's friends laid the brick. It's twenty-six feet in diameter, about half the size of my Prairie Moon labyrinth. Very different energies. You'll feel it when you walk them."

Sharon and I retraced our steps past a barn and raised beds toward an acre of dried grass where Prairie Moon was located. Three black cows on the far side of a barbed wire fence stared with cool detachment.

"I have to tell you that my first labyrinth walk was a dud," she laughed. "It was a big Chartres pattern mowed in the grass in someone's backyard in Tulsa. I thought I was supposed to have some kind of illuminating experience, but nothing happened. It was *coyote medicine,* a trickster who shows you a lesson. That taught me to not be so serious, to lighten up. Now when I walk, it's like the energy of the labyrinth enriches everything."

Four tall, slender poles wrapped in different colored strips of fabric (red, blue, yellow and black/white) marked the cardinal directions around Prairie Moon's fifty-foot path.

"When I asked the land where to put another labyrinth in 2000," Sharon said, "my dowsing pendulum led me to an energy vortex on this spot. After I spray-painted the design, I put out a call to women to help me lay the brick. Twenty-one showed up on the evening of the summer solstice. We walked to the center and said prayers. Monty, a Lakota medicine man, blessed it."

Sharon stood erect at the labyrinth's entrance, the stiff wind whipping her white hair like the tails on the fabric poles. "This labyrinth has absorbed energy, and pain, from people who have walked it." she reflected. "The earth takes and holds what humans deposit."

"Will you walk Prairie Moon with me?" I asked.

"I let people walk by themselves. I'm a *way-show-er.* I provide a place for people to walk. Just be sure to pay attention to what's on the path and what's around you. Whatever you experience is what your walk is supposed to be."

Prairie Moon's powerful energy pushed me forward in a twirling dance, while minutes later Well's quiet presence slowed my pace to a meditative walk. I had felt the personality of the land through the soles of my feet. It felt akin to my own.

MILES DOWN THE interstate, Michael started reading again. "After six and a half bumpy hours on two flights ... I [am] finally landing in Oklahoma, where it indeed feels as if the wind is sweeping down our plane." What do you know? He has been to Oklahoma.

6

New Life and New Heights

West Virginia, Virginia, Delaware

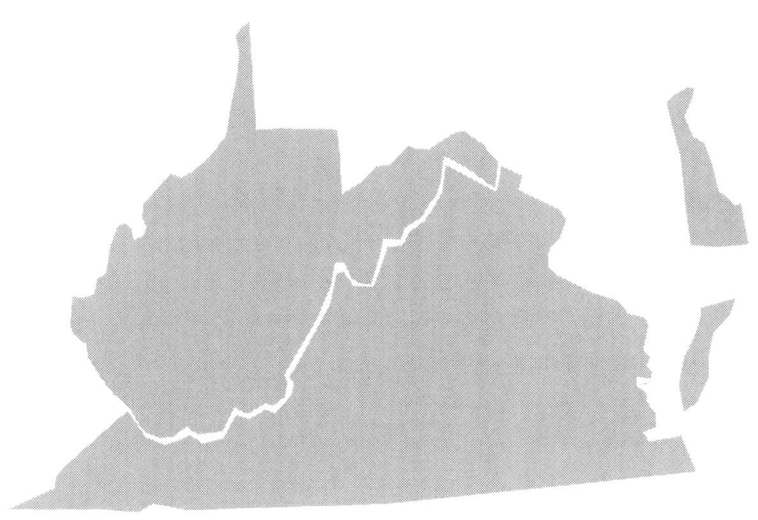

Top, left to right: Susan Wisniewski, West Virginia; Sharon Harris, Delaware. Bottom: Jeanne Russell, Virginia.

~ Twylla's journal ~

On the train from Grand Central Station
to Tarrytown Station, New York
February 13, 2013

KATHERINE'S PREGNANT! SHE just called and said that she and Andy had "some news."

"Are you sitting down?" she asked. Of course, I knew. You don't ask your mother if she's sitting down to tell her that you bought a new car, got a raise, or cooked a perfect batch of vegetarian chili.

"Yes, I'm on the train to meet Marian. What's up?" I asked, trying my best to sound clueless.

"We're going to have a baby!"

"AAAAAAA!!!" I screamed, ignoring the fifty-six other people on the train eavesdropping on our conversation. That's so exciting!"

"Yeah, pretty crazy, huh? I just took the pregnancy test this morning, and it came out positive. The baby should be born sometime in October. Can you believe you'll have five grandchildren?"

It's not the five grandchildren I can't believe; it's that Katherine, our youngest, is having a baby. She'll be twenty-seven when the baby is born. Twenty-seven. I can still picture her at four, reaching up for my hand as we walked, hearing her sweet voice say, "I love you."

In nine months my little girl will be a mother.

It's a lot to take in — a lot of WONDERFUL!

Susan Wisniewski
Shepherdstown, West Virginia
February 13, 2013

SUSAN GREETED MARIAN and me at the front door of her two-story saltbox and led us through the house to the back deck, where we reentered misty drizzle.

"The labyrinth is directly below us," she said, pointing across the sloping backyard to a circle of closely-spaced cedars around the labyrinth's perimeter. Exiting steps to the side, we came face-to-face with the last thing I expected—a second labyrinth.

"You have two labyrinths?" I asked. Only one is listed on the Labyrinth Locator."

"I always wanted to have a Chartres and classical," Susan explained, "so I built this one about five years ago. I call it my Barefoot Labyrinth."

We walked past a perfectly manicured grass-and-paver seven-circuit labyrinth. Its uniquely squared turns looked like the corners of a mouth locked in a permanent smile. I smiled back.

"It's hard to believe that our Chartres labyrinth is eighteen years old," Susan reflected. "We got the idea to build it in 1993 when my husband, Michael, and our three children visited an Iron Age kingdom in Lejre, Denmark. I had studied there in college, and it's where I walked my first labyrinth. One day we were wandering over the grounds and topped a hill where we discovered a beautiful stone spiral. We walked it together, which was a really sweet family moment. It had an energy about it like people had danced and prayed around it and had connected to the earth long ago."

Susan stopped between two cairns that marked the labyrinth entrance. "This was the only spot in the backyard that wasn't claimed for something else. Michael and I both liked the Chartres design. Something about it having four quadrants appealed to us. We found the plans on the internet."

The labyrinth spread before us, an immense sea of blonde grasses drained of their color one frosty morning months before. Drained of color, but not energy.

Intense energy radiated from it, much like Sharon's Prairie Moon labyrinth in Oklahoma where I had danced. Susan's labyrinth invited me to run as fast as I could. I would, later.

"We needed to locate the center for this roughly one hundred-foot space," Susan continued, "so we dowsed for it, each in our own way. Michael used traditional dowsing rods. I used muscle-checking, and we came up with the same answer, the same place of energy."

"Can you explain how that works?" I asked.

"In traditional dowsing," Susan explained, "the person holds two dowsing rods in front of him and repeats a sentence or question. Michael walked the area and stated, 'This is the best place to center the labyrinth.' The rods stayed separate until he got a YES, then they swung towards one another and crossed over like an X. I repeated the same statement as I crossed the yard while muscle checking. I formed a loop with the thumb and pointer finger of one hand, then used the other pointer finger to sweep through the inside of that loop. If the finger breaks through the loop, the answer is NO. If it cannot break the loop, the answer is YES."

We stepped directly across the path to the labyrinth's center. A fairy, about the size of a small cat, reclined delicately in a ring of rocks. Her flowing, off-the-shoulder Grecian gown matched the dark gray of her patinated body.

"This fairy and the one on the lower edge of the labyrinth acknowledge the unseen world of Earth Spirits, to help us remember their presence, watching and helping us. The one down there is a permanent memorial to my dear friend who passed away over three years ago," Susan shared.

Following a moment of silence, she continued. "Every time I walk this labyrinth I have a different experience. I walk it to pray and get answers, to buoy and strengthen me, to exercise and get fresh air. I used to be very strict. If I walked in, I had to walk out. But I've given myself permission to just go one way when I don't have time for both.

"I walk the Barefoot Labyrinth more often since it's right outside the door and easy. Usually in the morning, especially in the summer, I'll walk it barefoot. It takes me about five minutes in and out so I sometimes call it my Five-Minute Labyrinth," she laughed.

"Walk them both. They're quite different."

Again, I thought of Sharon, who had described her labyrinths with almost the exact words. Both women had spoken of dowsing, of Earth Spirits, of the land's energy. Women, separated by over a thousand miles, shared distinct callings to create two labyrinths on their land.

Distinct, yet kindred spirits.

Jeanne Russell
Edinburg, Virginia
February 14, 2013

"My house is right on Main Street so if you can find Edinburg, you can find my house," began Jeanne's simple directions on the World Wide Labyrinth Locator. Marian spied the house. I noticed the rocks. It was an orderly line of run-of-the-mill rocks, running the length of Jeanne's front yard. Nothing extraordinary. Yet something about their thoughtful placement seemed significant.

Jeanne opened the front door before we had a chance to knock. "You're here! You made it. Come on in," she said, waving us out of the cold into her sunny 1900-era living room. "I know you want to see the labyrinth so let's do that first, then we'll come back in for tea and muffins. I've been so excited for you to come!"

We tiptoed around patches of lingering snow, in and out of filtered sunlight. What first appeared to be a parade of stalled turtles turned out to be rocks lining Jeanne's classical labyrinth, five circuits rather than the traditional seven.

"My vision is to have a secret garden back here," Jeanne explained as she led us single file into the labyrinth. "In the spring that bramble of bushes over there is filled with yellow forsythia flowers, and that tree's a lilac. It smells heavenly. I have plans for an arbor."

With one hand outstretched to her side, Jeanne traced the rocks as we circled the path. "Friends brought me these rocks. I sent out an email saying, 'I'm going to build a labyrinth. I need stones about the size of my hands. Please bring me rocks.' And they did, enough for the whole labyrinth! At first I didn't know how in the world to make it, but I found the directions on the internet. I tied a string around a stake in the center, marked the path, then laid rocks along the lines.

"After it was finished," she went on, "I sent out another email inviting my friends to a labyrinth party. My friend, Kim, created a ceremony then we all walked. It was a magical evening."

Jeanne's animated pace and narrative stopped as abruptly as she did. Marian and I pulled up inches behind, avoiding a three-way collision in the labyrinth's center.

"This bench belonged to my grandparents. I loved them dearly." Jeanne sat for a moment gently rubbing the curved armrest, now green with layered years. "Sometimes when I step into the labyrinth, I'm thinking about my problems or tensions in my life. Then I'll sit on this bench and breathe. I'll sit here as long as I need to. I hear the birds and smell nature, especially the flowers if they're in bloom. It helps me become centered."

We all paused to breathe in winter's freshness like sheets newly plucked from a clothesline. A gray squirrel darted across the damp ground and up the side of a tree. A dog barked in the distance.

"You know who really loved this labyrinth?" she laughed. "Penelope, my cat. I even named the labyrinth after her. At the end of the blessing ceremony, Penelope purred *meow* to give it her own blessing. Sadly, she died. But I find other cats around it all the time, walking on it and laying on it. I've heard that animals feel the labyrinth's energy."

Back in the dining room, Jeanne introduced us to Penelope's successor, black-and-white-splotched Louie Louie who snoozed undisturbed as we sipped Earl Grey. The red tablecloth matched a large red-petaled flower Jeanne had painted on the wall.

"It's just one of the creative things I like to do," she said. "I make feng shui mandalas, design websites, do freelance writing and participate in the local theater productions. I get some of my most amazing ideas when I walk the labyrinth. They usually come to me as I walk out. When my livelihood depends on creative ideas, it's like a secret weapon. In hard times I sometimes forget about the labyrinth, but when you're too busy is exactly when you should make the time to walk it."

Then almost as an afterthought, she added, "You know, when you build a labyrinth you make it your own. My community of friends adds so much meaning to my labyrinth. Did I tell you that some people wrote their names on the bottoms of the rocks they brought? Someone etched *Penelope's Rock* on one. What they brought into the labyrinth reflects them, and I feel supported by them as I walk and in my life."

Rocks. Placed with intention and infused with connection. Marian backed out of the driveway and eased onto Main Street. Those run-of-the mill rocks? Anything but ordinary.

Sharon Harris
Milton, Delaware
February 15, 2013

VISITING LAVENDER FIELDS in February is a bit like vacationing at a ski resort in July, not the best timing. But Marian and I didn't follow the purple sign to Warrington Manor Lavender Fields for the lavender. (Although a sprig would have been nice to tuck in our pillows.) We were there to hear Sharon's story. Why, in the midst of a five-acre lavender farm, did she build a labyrinth?

"Welcome to our farmhouse!" Sharon said with a firm handshake and gentle smile as she opened the door and took our jackets. "This is Marie Mayor who owns the farm with me."

"How about a cup of tea?" Marie asked. "It's lavender, of course."

"Thanks! I've never tried any," Marian answered.

"Neither have I," I said, "but it's exactly what I'd expect at a farm that has thirty-seven varieties of over three thousand lavender plants." Sharon and Marie gave me a puzzled look, so I quickly added, "I read your website."

"This stylish home isn't quite what comes to mind when I picture a farmhouse," Marian said between sips of tea.

"Well, believe me," Sharon chuckled, "it was not a pretty sight when we bought it in 2002. This farmhouse is built over the foundation of a previous one that dated to the 1890s. But there was something about this place from the very beginning. It really did speak to me. I thought maybe it was the country air. I love being outside. It's not just me, though. People come here and I hear them say it over and over, 'This place is magical.' "

"And this farm is more than lavender. It's about creating space and community," Marie added. "We're kind of like a cottage industry, providing jobs for people. Women work in the gift shop. People create items to be sold in the gift shop. A lady makes stained glass, while another grows vegetables in our garden and gives them away. Book groups meet in our restored barn, and couples get married in our labyrinth."

"It seems like I've always known about labyrinths. High school might have been the first time," Sharon noted. "I wasn't really drawn to them, just knew about them. Then when I was attending a retreat at Kirkridge Retreat Center in Pennsylvania, I saw a finger labyrinth. The idea popped into my head, 'I can do this! I can build a labyrinth on our land!' I thought women, particularly, would enjoy walking a labyrinth when they came to visit the lavender."

After refills of tea, Sharon offered to take us on a tour of the farm. She saved the labyrinth for the final stop, inviting us to follow her under a wooden arbor into a circle of dried lavender plants and cryptomeria trees.

"I had to clear the land first before I could start building the labyrinth, so I rented a Bobcat," Sharon said matter-of-factly. "When the man delivered it, he asked if I knew how to use it. I said, 'Yes!' then figured it out after he left. It wouldn't start at first, but once I put on the seat belt, no problem.

"It took me about six months to build, from the fall of 2005 to the spring of 2006. I put a metal stake in the middle, attached a rope and made a circle. I outlined the quadrants with orange spray paint then started in the center and worked out from there, one quadrant at a time. To keep weeds down I laid down pebbles for the path, but I'm not entirely satisfied with them."

Sharon kicked a brick with the toe of her boot. "I found discarded bricks from all around the farm to outline the path. I dug an eleven-inch trench and laid each brick by hand, all myself. It actually was peaceful working out here, especially listening to the sounds of birds and snow geese flying over."

Sharon made it sound easy. It wasn't, of course. It was all in the attitude.

"I hardly walk it myself," she offered. "I built it for others to walk. It makes me happy to build something that people are getting so much out of. People do their own thing in the labyrinth. I even see people out here at night walking it with flashlights. I've had people tell me that it's a life-changing experience. I don't quite understand that. I take care of the flowers and the lavender around it. I weed it."

Marian joined Sharon and Marie for another cup of tea, leaving me alone to walk. White stones clicked under my shoes. I rounded the first turn when my phone rang. I had forgotten to silence it, thankfully. It was Katherine.

We walked together, as if arm in arm, and spoke of new life.

EN ROUTE

Manhattan apartment
February 15, 2013

I HATE HEIGHTS, HATE them! So why did I have to be the one driving from Sharon's this afternoon when the hump of the Delaware Memorial Bridge materialized out of thin air? I looked for a place to pull over and switch places with Marian, but traffic swarmed on all sides. There was no way out.

Then paralyzing cold began to overtake my body. It blocked my peripheral vision, shut down my hearing, stiffened my fingers around the steering wheel and forced my regular breaths into rapid-fire bullets.

My eyes magnified one inch of highway at a time, the only inch I could manage. I started to mumble. "I can do this. I can do this. I can do this."

Closing in on the highest point, I squeezed the panic as far away from my head as possible, into my chest, stomach, toes. My brain knew that the edge was feet away, that if I turned my head I would see it. And I would die. Or that everything would turn black. It felt like the same thing.

My mumblings must have become louder. Marian leaned forward so that her face appeared in my limited field of vision. Her mouth moved.

I heard nothing.

"I can do this. I can do this."

The end of the bridge appeared as a narrow tunnel with only a pinprick of light poking through. I aimed the car in its direction.

"Twylla, are you OK? Are you OK? You look as pale as a sheet."

Marian's voice. I heard it as the faintest edge of a whisper, but I heard it.

I pulled over somewhere. I don't remember where.

Marian took over. "I was so worried about you. It was like you were a zombie or something. What happened?"

I tried to explain but talking took effort. I needed to sit and let energy return. I leaned my head back and breathed.

I can't do that again. No more bridges, NO more heights. I'll drive on flat ground only. But the rest of the United States isn't totally flat and isn't all ground!

How will I get better at this? How?

7

Across the Golden Gate to Mt. Shasta

California, Oregon

Left: Lani Rossetta, Oregon. Above: Mary Grove, California.

~ Twylla's journal ~

On a flight from La Guardia to San Francisco International
March 12, 2013

By now, Drew's found a copy of the itinerary that I hurriedly stuck on the fridge at 3 a.m. under one of Mickey Mouse's magnetized shoes. Together they can check on my progress each morning as Drew reaches for his yogurt.

Early on in my travels, Margie said, "When you visit a labyrinth on the west coast, let me know. I'll try to fly down and go with you." An extremely generous offer, considering that it's 1,500-plus miles from Juneau to San Francisco; yet our rendezvous feels predestined. After all, Margie is the friend who introduced me to labyrinths almost a decade ago. Now, she's joining me on a labyrinth-inspired journey. It could be no other way.

* * *

Lani Rossetta
Central Point, Oregon
March 14, 2013

THE CASCADE RANGE appeared a hazy blue through the early morning sun as Margie and I pulled up in front of Lani's hilltop house. "You'll get a sweeping view of the valley from the labyrinth," Lani had written in an email. "It's a modified Baltic Wheel." I had never heard of one.

"I've answered your four questions already," Lani smiled, handing me two pages, stapled, with the heading Labyrinth Questions Answered by Lani Rossetta. I put down my cup of tea and leafed through them.

Super-organized. Prepared ahead of time. A kid-friendly labyrinth, handmade of cloth-covered beads on the kitchen table. I had to ask the obvious question. "Are you a teacher?"

"I have been," she laughed. "Now, I'm an occupational therapist plus a Reiki master and yoga instructor.

"I made this when I was an OT in the local schools," Lani said as she picked up the labyrinth from the table. "I was working with children who had fine motor difficulties and wheelchair mobility issues when I got the idea to connect them with labyrinths. I thought the interaction would improve their attention, memory, fine/gross motor, cognitive, and directional/spatial skills. I taught kids how to make finger labyrinths like this one and others out of cotton balls, magnets on cookie sheets, buttons and paper clips. You name it. Then they tried to trace the path without touching the edges or crossing the border."

Lani referred to a book she had written, *Labyrinths for Kids.* "Most of my ideas are in here. This section is about labyrinths I built outdoors for children to walk and maneuver in wheelchairs. You'll see that some are constructed from strings of lights, long pieces of rope, even straws and plastic spoons stuck in the soil. It was fun for them and me, plus they made progress.

"My labyrinth's just out the back door," she said. "I'll tell you more out there."

I stood on the deck overlooking Lani's labyrinth, puzzling over what was unique about the Baltic design. As my eyes focused on the whole rather than its parts, a woman's figure materialized with her white, pebbled gown extending from entrance to center.

"You're right!" Lani exclaimed when I voiced my impression. "A Baltic Wheel is also known as a goddess labyrinth. Instead of having a common entrance and exit, a Baltic has two openings. The path to the left is a more winding route to the center and back out; the one to the right is more direct. Unlike the Chartres and classical labyrinths, you can reach the center and exit without retracing your steps."

With camera in hand, Lani positioned herself on a stack of flat rocks at the entrance, clearly eager for Margie and me to walk her labyrinth. As Margie stepped to the left and I to the right, she snapped pictures and continued her story.

"My husband, Stan, hauled I don't know how many wheelbarrow loads of rocks—probably six or seven pickups full—and I laid them along the path. That was after we staked the center and tied a rope to it. I marked the path with a two-foot board.

"When you get to the center, notice the chunks of obsidian. They neutralize negativity. And, Twylla, you're about to pass the quartz we picked up on our trip to Arkansas." I couldn't miss the dazzling conglomerate of crystals from my home state, fused together eons ago into what looked more like jewelry than geology.

"The rocks get jumbled sometimes by deer that nose out acorns from beneath them. And we always know that wild turkeys have paid us a visit when we find their droppings along the path."

Lani laughed while Margie and I checked our shoes. We completed the remainder of our joint walk in silence, returning to the hem of the goddess' dress. Lani asked us to pose for a picture at the round stepping stone in the center, or goddess' head.

"I'm glad you walked together," she said. "I love to walk the labyrinth with friends. I've held full moon ceremonies here and friends have brought drums so we can drum our way through. I walk it alone to meditate and sometimes I even run it. My grandkids walk with me, and we play games and do art in the labyrinth. The labyrinth's greatest value to me has been my work with children."

I looked back at the goddess as Margie and I walked to the car. Her outstretched arms felt like Lani's encircling invitation to share the walk. Family, friends, wildlife and children, especially children, would always be welcome in her labyrinth . . . as were two women on a journey.

Mary Grove
Piedmont, California
March 15, 2013

MARY'S NEIGHBORHOOD WAS a mixture of old and new California with mission style bungalows, colonials and contemporary—all bordered by hedges, shrubs, trees and perfectly manicured lawns. Parking in front of Mary's house, Margie and I had no way of knowing how the surrounding area had played a part in her decision to build a labyrinth.

We followed Mary into a sitting area by the front window where a pot of tea waited on the coffee table. A rose-colored camellia blossom brushed against the window pane.

"My first labyrinth experience was about an hour from here at Mercy Center in Burlingame," Mary began. "I spent a month there doing Spiritual Direction training and walked the labyrinth a lot, especially while I was working on a sermon for Mary Magdalene Day. I was preaching for the first time."

"Are you clergy?" I asked.

"I went to Episcopal seminary for two years but had to quit because of health issues, as you can see from my crutches. I have Lyme disease. I continue with my Spiritual Direction work, which is hugely important in terms of staying in conversation with people. It has become more difficult for me to hold onto thoughts when I'm writing, but the talking I can still do."

Mary commented about her illness without hesitation or elaboration. Wanting to acknowledge it in some way, Margie and I simultaneously said a variation of "I'm sorry" and waited for Mary to continue.

"The labyrinth at Mercy Center is outdoors and that made a huge difference for me. I really liked the meditative base and the controlled kind of movement that lets you completely let go of barriers and boundaries that you usually hold. I wanted to share it, so I decided to build one here. In a neighborhood where people are often very concerned about privacy, the labyrinth breaks that up a bit."

Mary gestured toward the dining room windows. "The labyrinth is below those windows at the end of the driveway. I only had a small triangular-shaped space about seventeen feet across where I could build it. I got out my big book about labyrinths by Herman Kerr and found a Baltic design that I thought I could alter."

"A Baltic?" I exclaimed. "We walked a Baltic yesterday in Oregon, our first."

"That is a coincidence because you don't see them very often. If I put a classical labyrinth in that space, you could walk it in two minutes; but with the Baltic, you can keep going and going until you decide to finish.

"My friend, Daniel Green, and his friend, Carlos, helped me with the heavy work," she explained. "We needed a backhoe to even out the space; but the rest of the work was done by hand, which was really important to me.

"I loved choosing rocks for it," she continued. "They have such presence. Arrival matters in a labyrinth, so I selected a piece of five-sided Canadian basalt for the center. Since there's not much space in the center, we placed a Yucca River rock to the side for people to sit on. The pebbles I chose for the path are a rich mixture of earth tones.

"Follow me and I'll show it to you from the window."

As we admired the labyrinth from above, every detail matched the scene in my imagination, except one. "Mary, I didn't realize that your labyrinth is connected directly to the sidewalk."

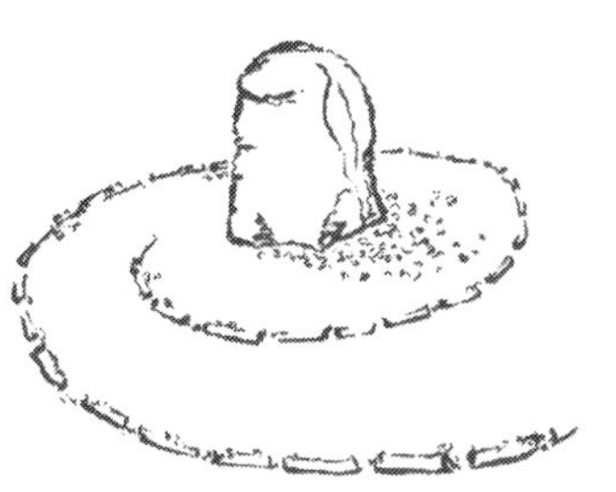

"I designed it that way so anyone walking by can come in. I think that walls and fences, which act as boundaries, are painful to the earth. The more we can pick away at that, the better. That was my hope for the land out there, that it would become a shared sort of centering space. Now that I can no longer walk it, I love watching others walk it. There are two boys, one four and the other eight, who come by often. They run the path in a way that's easy and full of light."

Mary handed me a set of stapled papers from the table. "Here is a copy of the Labyrinth Blessing I wrote for the dedication. I hope you find it meaningful."

She walked with us to the front door where we said goodbye. "Blessings on the rest of your journey," she said with a gentle smile.

Margie settled onto the Yucca River rock while I circled the short distance to the center and unfolded Mary's blessing. Leaning against the gray basalt, I read the opening line.

" ... Receive the work of our hands in this place, and the friendship of those gathered to bless it, and make this labyrinth your gift to all who come here ... ."

If Mary were looking out her window, she would be smiling.

* * *

~ Twylla's Journal ~

Sanctuary
Grace Cathedral, San Francisco
March 15, 2013

THIS IMMENSE GOTHIC cathedral is dark, except for the overhead lights along the center aisle and votive candles outlining the labyrinth. Harp music and Tibetan bells sound softly at the edge of the darkness. Ten people are still walking, their feet noiseless as they pass one another. I was one of the first to enter and am now sitting at the end of a pew, journaling, the way I've come to process most everything in my life.

The cathedral is entirely ours for the evening. It's the end of our first full day of the workshop, "The Emerging Spirituality: The Awakened Self," taught by the Rev. Dr. Lauren Artress. Lauren brought the labyrinth to Grace Cathedral in 1991; in fact, she almost singlehandedly re-introduced the labyrinth into Western culture. Since then, interest in labyrinths has snowballed and Lauren has crisscrossed the world sharing it with people. Not that those of us she's training as labyrinth facilitators will be "Lauren clones," but we will allow her influence to be felt simultaneously in hundreds of places.

I wish I could say that my reason for registering for this training was based purely on my interest in labyrinths, but it was more practical than that. I thought that being a facilitator would give me credibility as I continue this journey and write the book about it. "Twylla Alexander, Veriditas Certified Labyrinth Facilitator." I expected to learn about the labyrinth, not be touched by it. I was wrong, of course.

A bench across from Grace Cathedral
March 16, 2013

I ENCIRCLED THE labyrinth with the other walkers last night after the final person finished. We stood in silence. The harps and bells had quieted. The only sounds were the whispers of our own internal reflections. I've walked many labyrinths in the last year, each very different. But my experience last night was pivotal. I felt it in the turns, my favorite part of the Chartres labyrinth, especially the tight turns, the ones that follow one another quickly toward the center. I felt the rhythm of the labyrinth in my body. The design at my feet was no longer a separate entity but an integral part of my life ... somehow absorbed into who I am, or am becoming.

This morning Lauren read a paragraph from her book *The Sacred Path Companion.* It was as if she were reading it solely to me.

> "I am amazed by the number of people who begin to find their life's purpose and shape their life's work through walking the labyrinth. It is certainly true of me, and I have seen many others whose gifts are opened, whether it be teaching, organizing, writing, or speaking. It is as though the labyrinth 'births' people into their gifts. This does not happen without taking risks, of course, but the unfolding of people's lives is quite dramatic when this powerful archetypal energy is activated. You are freed to take courageous action on your own behalf."

"... [T]o take courageous action on your own behalf." These words could be my mantra, one I didn't even know I was looking for... until today.

8

Spanish Moss and Pine Needles

North Carolina, Georgia, South Carolina

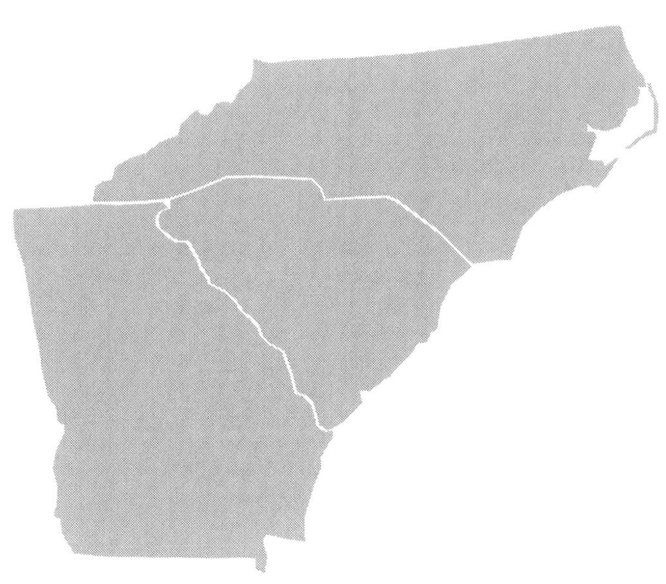

Top, left to right: Catherine Anderson, North Carolina; Helen Rivers, South Carolina. Right: Nancy Hartness, Georgia.

~ Twylla's Journal ~

LaGuardia Airport, NYC
April 19, 2013

GERI AND I sip tea and share an enormous airport muffin, the kind that spills over the edge of the paper liner, as equally delicious as it is unhealthy. Our flight to Charlotte departs in forty-five minutes.

Geri, another Juneau friend, is going with me on this leg of my journey. I haven't even calculated the number of miles from Juneau to New York City, then on to North Carolina/South Carolina/Georgia and reverse. Alaska folks don't make decisions to travel based on miles, though. Everywhere is far from Alaska.

When we discovered that Geri's dates to visit me in NYC overlapped with the next labyrinth trip, she said, "I'd love to go with you and learn about your journey. Plus I've never been to the South."

How could I have known when Geri introduced herself as Katherine's first-grade teacher that she would become my friend, and still be my friend, twenty years later? And that she would say yes to a journey that isn't her own like Marian and Margie before her ... because she cares.

I learn from my friends how to be a friend.

Catherine Anderson
Charlotte, North Carolina
April 19, 2013

DAFFODILS, AZALEAS, DOGWOOD, redbud, camellia. I rolled down the rental car window to inhale spring in the South and was greeted by a blast of familiar humidity. The only piece of the picture that didn't match was Catherine's greeting.

"Hi! I've been looking for you!" she said, without a trace of a southern accent. Australian perhaps?

"It's such a lovely morning, and there's still some dew on the grass. I wondered if you'd want to walk the labyrinth first. If you take off your shoes, the walk will be especially delightful. But there's tea and goodies in my studio too, so you pick," Catherine offered, as she led us into her backyard.

"I've never walked a labyrinth, so I'll let you decide," Geri answered.

I was shocked! Never walked a labyrinth? How could I have missed this key piece of information?

"Well, aren't you lucky?" laughed Catherine. "You have two labyrinth facilitators on hand to launch your first walk. I tell people to make it their own, walk at their own pace. It's a different experience for each person. The same path will take you in, then back out. You can't get lost."

Half an hour later, Geri and I joined Catherine at a long wooden table in her art studio. "So how was your first walk?" she asked.

"Very peaceful, even the grass tickling my feet," Geri smiled. "But I do have a question. Did you actually build it yourself?"

"I did, with my son's help," Catherine explained. "I'm sure it looked rather comical when he was running around in circles spray-painting the ground. The only thing that I didn't take into account was that grass would grow in the spring and cover up the whole thing. My husband took pity on me and dug a trench where the spray paint had been, and we filled in with white stones to mark the circles.

"It's not exactly perfect but life isn't perfect either. It's the experience you have walking it, not whether it's a perfect labyrinth."

Catherine pointed to a spot beside the studio door. "I taped a photograph of the Chartres Cathedral labyrinth right there, years before we actually built mine. It was the first labyrinth I ever saw. Every time I was here working, I'd look at the photo, then look out the window and visualize the labyrinth in my backyard. I just had a sense that I had to have one there. I can't explain why. Sometimes I don't even walk it; I simply look at it. There's something about the design being there."

She paused to sip her tea, and I asked the question I had been wondering since we met, "Catherine, where are you from?"

"Oh, my accent," she smiled. "I was born and raised in South Africa and moved to Charlotte with my husband and two children.

"You know, it's interesting to think back on that transition. I was an attorney in South Africa but made a conscious decision to be creative when we came here. That led to my photography business, which was not what I really wanted to do. But sometimes I think we have to go through these rites of passage to learn what we need to learn, before we can go to the next stage."

Surrounded by enough art supplies to fill a store, I didn't need a sign to spell out the significance of creativity in Catherine's life. One hung on the wall, none the less: CREATE in bold black letters followed by five definitions.

"It's like the pilgrimage we're all on, isn't it?" she wondered aloud. "I'm constantly re-evaluating. I ask myself, 'Am I still headed in the right direction?' Yet I know that it's not about right and wrong. I may not have every part of a plan worked out but begin taking steps toward where I want to be. For me, it's about living life intentionally."

She pulled a book from the shelf and flipped through the pages. "The labyrinth sometimes helps me figure out what to do next, like when I was stuck in the process of writing this book, *The Creative Photographer*. I was in the center of the labyrinth when the words came to me, 'You just need to make a list.' It sounded so basic, but I walked out and knew what to do. It's a tool to access your inner wisdom, what's within you."

Catherine handed us each a small, wooden disc with a labyrinth printed on one side. "I invite walkers to write an intention before they walk or a remembrance afterwards."

I carried mine outside, sat on the bench beside the labyrinth and wrote:

Nancy Hartness
Athens, Georgia
April 20, 2013

NANCY'S ENTRY ON the World Wide Labyrinth Locator intrigued me. It was the photo of a red shoe I couldn't resist—a single red shoe with stockinged foot—stepping into a labyrinth, followed by the description:

> "Classical labyrinth in rectangular shape ... more organic than perfect and symmetrical ... but it is a generous labyrinth in spirit."

I sensed that its creator was a generous and adventurous spirit. Anyone who wears red shoes is.

"You're the first person to express an interest in my labyrinth since I put in on the Locator," Nancy said as she and her husband, Charlie, ushered Geri and me to the dining table. "I wasn't walking it that much before you wrote. In fact, I considered pulling it up. We had taken down our big tree in the front yard, close to the labyrinth, so the whole area had a different feel to it. But your email re-enthused me.

"Then last night," she said with a slight hesitation, "I dreamed, more like had a premonition, that you wouldn't like my labyrinth. Of course, now that you're here and I'm awake, I'm totally fine with it!"

Although being the central character in anyone's nightmare is a bit unsettling, I understood Nancy's apprehension. Sharing any creation is a risk, especially with a stranger who wants to pass it on to the rest of the world. I felt honored and responsible, and told her so.

"The labyrinth you'll see in our front yard isn't the one I wanted at first," Nancy explained. "I wanted a Chartres style like the first one I walked in Bellevue, Washington and the one at Grace Cathedral in San Francisco. It was while I was walking the one at Grace that I felt the labyrinth tell me to build one of my own, here. I researched and measured, but we didn't have the space in our yard. I was really frustrated because the labyrinth told me to build one and I couldn't."

"I suggested that she build this kind," Charlie added, pointing to Nancy's needle felted seven-circuit labyrinth on the table. "I told her that if she really liked it, she could transpose the design and size to somewhere in the yard."

"So with fear and trembling," Nancy responded, "I took Charlie's advice and drew a labyrinth with sidewalk chalk on our parking pad behind the house."

"With fear and trembling?" I wondered.

"I thought I might not get it right, you know, that feeling of wanting it to be perfect. But it was fun! I wrote poems on the path—one about cicadas singing—and decorated the middle with spirals and designs. Then when construction guys covered up our parking pad, I built the one in the front."

We carried our glasses of ginger-peach tea to the front porch and gazed down on Nancy's labyrinth. Covered half in bright sunlight and half in the house's shadow, it took a few seconds for the labyrinth's orange outline to come into focus.

"I started staking out the shape with some prickly twine and nails I had on hand, but the lines wouldn't stay curved. They just wouldn't. I thought that maybe I needed two-inch nails or something, but I didn't have that many. So I finally decided that the labyrinth wanted to be more squarish or rectangular-ish in its imperfect way ... its perfectly imperfect way."

Wearing her red Mary Janes, Nancy took a long, deliberate step into the labyrinth.

"Sometimes I walk because it's a beautiful morning," she shared, "and the labyrinth slows me down enough to notice new leaves on a tree or a bird chirping. It's an intentional kind of walking. After I finish, I turn and thank the labyrinth for the gift of itself."

Geri and I followed on the narrow, slightly sloping path, stopping to read Nancy's handmade signs.

My favorite was on a shovel blade, its simple white letters asking profoundly wise questions:

Life is Short
Where you Been?
Where You Goin'?
Think About It

Geri singled out an octagonal piece of metal displaying the familiar phrase often attributed to St. Augustine:

It Is Solved By Walking

"We have a gift for you," Nancy said after our walk. We followed them back into the house where Charlie picked up a fiddle and Nancy a banjo. "Twylla, since you're from Arkansas, we want to play a tune for you and Geri, 'Echoes of the Ozarks.'"

For the next few minutes, their music filled the room and floated through the open windows. It was mountain music that begged a story—not a perfect story—just one filled with the warmth of a shared afternoon among friends.

Helen Rivers
Lexington, South Carolina
April 21, 2013

A THREE-FOOT TIN man fashioned from paint cans, soup cans, your-guess-is-as-good-as-mine cans, pointed our way from Helen's front yard to a gate around the corner.

"Welcome to my backyard garden," Helen said opening a wooden gate to reveal a world as magical as Disney's. "The labyrinth's in the far back. I'll give you a tour on our way."

A fuchsia chandelier hung from a tree, its light bulbs replaced by teacups and saucers. Raised flowerbeds looked inviting enough to sleep in, with their freshly painted white headboards and footboards.

I'm a Master Gardener," Helen explained, "and I like to make things from just about anything I have around or that someone drops off in my front yard. I was in corporate America for years, marketing, and got stymied. This is lots more fun! I think that the trouble with our lives now is that we're so busy going somewhere to get something done that we don't take time to notice things around us."

We followed a curving outline of upside down flower pots, past a clawfoot tub of irises toward the labyrinth. The sweet smell of tea olive blossoms floated from nearby bushes.

"I love to look at the flowers as I walk the labyrinth," Helen smiled. "I walk it twice a day in good weather, in the morning to pull weeds because I can't see a weed and not pull it, then in the afternoon for myself. It's very relaxing for me because I'm a control freak and it helps lower my stress level. Back here, I don't hear all that traffic out on the road, not once I get walking."

She led us to a bench in the labyrinth's center, encircled by bamboo stalks. "When I built the labyrinth, I planned for this sixteen-foot center so I could install a water orb and bench. I enjoy hearing the sound of water cascading while I sit here."

Helen resumed her story—more softly than before—as all three of us sat in the center, soothed by water and stillness. "I walked my first labyrinth, a canvas one, at our church here in Lexington. I walked it and was hooked. I wanted to put one in our yard, so I did some research. I located a man named Sam Richardson in Asheville, North Carolina who drew up plans to my requirements. He's a dowser and located the sweet spot for the center, then walked around asking Mother Earth where the entrance should be.

"It took me a year after that, though," she continued "to get ninety-three pine trees removed and the ground ready for layout. My husband delivered four dump truck loads of top soil and two loads of white sand. We put down eight layers of newspaper first, then the top soil and sand."

Helen shook her head. "I didn't think I'd ever get it finished. It took three years from conception to having it laid out and another three years to get it planted. The planting is on-going."

We left the center and walked along the path towards a lone red amaryllis. Helen bent over to touch it. "I don't know why I was supposed to build the labyrinth," she reflected. "I just know that God wanted me to. Someone is going to come one day that needs to hear Him and feel His presence, and they will. It's just kind of like in *Field of Dreams.* It said, 'Build this labyrinth,' and I said, 'I'm not gonna argue.' So I did!"

She took a step towards the house, then stopped. "I had a lady visit before the labyrinth was finished. The path wasn't smoothed out yet. After she walked, she shared that her husband had recently died. She said that walking the path helped her realize that life has its ups and downs and no matter how low the down, there is always a way up. You never know what people are going to experience.

"You go ahead and walk. I'll make us some sweet tea and lay out a few snacks."

Geri had walked ahead and paused on the labyrinth's outer ring in front of another of Helen's whimsical creations, a six-foot butterfly with pink fabric wings. I began my walk, but never finished. The sun and pine needles lulled me into deeper relaxation with each footstep. I sank to my knees, then gently settled onto my back, cradled by the labyrinth's path.

Feeling slightly self-conscious, I momentarily wondered what Helen might think about someone lying down in her labyrinth, but then recalled her words, "You never know what people are going to experience." I let my misgivings melt into the earth and closed my eyes.

EN ROUTE

Springbank Retreat Center
Kingstree, South Carolina
April 23, 2013

AFTER SCHEDULING HELEN'S labyrinth visit in Lexington, I Googled Springbank. Was it possible that this out-of-the-way retreat center, which had lived in my literary memory for over ten years, could be a doable side trip? I entered both locations on Google Maps and held my breath. One hour and forty-five minutes. Totally doable!

Sue Monk Kidd's book *The Dance of the Dissident Daughter* brought me here. I sat under a canopied circle of trees that Sue and her friend, Betty, discovered one night on their own personal journeys. From memory, I turned to page 102. Sentences were underlined, words starred. My handwriting filled the margins.

Sue wrote:

"I'd never done anything like this in my life, and I kept thinking how strange it would appear—two grown and proper women picking their way through the woods at night in search of—what?

" ... [W]e began to dance. I moved slowly around the circle of trees, around the fire, past the altar of stone and moss, then faster until my bare feet were pounding the ground. *Thump, thump, thump.* The sound landed in the silence with an untamed energy that was new to me but also recognizable and right, like feet staking out their ground, announcing their existence, stomping out of exile and coming home."

I imagined Geri and me trying to replicate Sue and Betty's experience, wandering through ink black woods, mistaking every other

tree root for a poisonous snake. I shook my head at the sight. No, copying their experience was never my intention.

But what was my intention? Why had I so vividly carried the image of this place in my consciousness all these years that I was compelled to come?

I let the questions hang among the Spanish moss while I turned the page and continued reading.

> "Before leaving Springbank, Betty and I walked back to the circle in the woods. Standing there in the clear light of morning, I knew I'd crossed a threshold."

> "... When a woman crosses a threshold, she knows that something inside her has shifted, if only slightly. She knows that she is on a different trajectory."

I had barely tiptoed onto my own path of self-discovery when I read Sue's book. Most of who I was, or thought I was, was based on a lifetime of shoulds and external expectations. I would have been hard-pressed to name my favorite color, much less recognize my own voice. Speaking my truth was miles and years down the road. I didn't know how to move forward, where to find the courage or inspiration to take the next step ... until the image of two women dancing around a fire, announcing their own existence, jumped off a page and ignited my imagination.

From that moment on, my trajectory was set. It came with no map of definites but rather with something much more enduring—a clear direction toward the woman I was meant to discover.

I know why I am here. Encircled by the same trees, standing in the same clearing as the women whose journeys immeasurably inspired my own, I close my eyes and whisper two words, "Thank you."

9

Into Middle Earth

Alabama

Lisa Kalloch, Alabama (right), with the author.

~Twylla's journal~

Grayton Beach, Florida
May 18, 2013

ONE YEAR AGO today I was in this exact spot, the same beach house, for a week-long holiday with daughter Elizabeth, son-in-law Ben, and granddaughter Ruby. I had already driven the twenty-five miles to Miramar Beach, walked Anne Hornstein's beach labyrinth and visited with her for two hours over multiple refills of tea.

"I did it. I made my first labyrinth visit!" I had shouted the minute I returned.

"Way to go, Grandmom!" Ruby shouted back, her hand positioned for a high-five. No matter that she didn't have a clue what a labyrinth is. It was all about sharing the moment.

Four days from now, I travel to state number twenty-one. I'm almost half-way to the end. My goal is to finish the next twenty-nine by July, 2014, fourteen months from now. July in Maui, Hawaii—number fifty. But the states get larger from here on out. I have no idea how I'll piece together visits in such far-flung places as Wyoming, Montana, Nevada, North and South Dakota.

I just know that I will. There's never been a moment in this past year that I've considered stopping. (Well, maybe for a fleeting moment on the highest point of the Delaware Memorial Bridge.) Sure, some of the planning has been tedious, even frustrating. But every time I've met another inspiring woman along the way, I've become enthused about the journey all over again. Now, my commitment to continue is shared. I'm carrying twenty women's stories with me, stories that have become a part of my own.

On to Citronelle, Alabama, three and a half hours away, where Lisa and Craig Kalloch own Middle Earth Healing and Learning Center. A forty-acre, "mostly natural demonstration site for sustainable practices" is where they built an outdoor grass labyrinth.

* * *

Lisa Kalloch
Citronelle, Alabama
May 22, 2013

I FELL INTO the rhythm of rural roads. Paved highways turned to dirt, brown then red.

The red dirt led me to a red house with a pitched roof of galvanized steel. In color and shape it resembled a barn, but with windows and front door much too stylish for animals. A sign hung to the right of the door ...

It is in OUR HANDS to create a better world for all who live in it.

"You came at a good time," Lisa said as she invited me into the house for a glass of water. "When you called last week, we were right in the middle of preparing for an aquaponics workshop, which we held the next day. Lots of work, but it went really well. I wanted to tell you all about the labyrinth that very minute, but I knew I couldn't let myself get sidetracked. Craig's waiting for us at the labyrinth. We both want to share it with you."

In the short walk from the house to a narrow trail leading to the labyrinth, the space abounded with evidence of Lisa and Craig's sustainable lifestyle. Lisa pointed out solar panels, rain barrels, greenhouse, vegetable and flowerbeds, barn and aquaponics system.

"That's our yurt," Lisa added as she gestured toward a large rounded tent with prayer flags hanging across the door. "We use it mainly as a classroom like when we teach an essential oils workshop."

Craig and three guineas greeted us at the labyrinth, an immense open space circled by pine trees or "guardian trees," as Craig referred to them.

"The labyrinth was the first change we made to this area when we moved here from Houston in 1999," Lisa said. "Because we follow the foundations of permaculture, we observed the land first and asked for divine guidance before moving forward. We knew that we were on a spiritual journey and that we had been guided here. We wanted the foundation of everything that would come forth to be spiritual. The labyrinth is the unifying presence here in Middle Earth, a oneness with the environment and all of creation."

"We built it within a year of arriving," Craig continued. "We walked around the woods, through shrubs and trees as I carried my pendulum and asked, 'Is this the place for the labyrinth?' For me, the pendulum moves in a circle when the answer is Yes. When I reached this spot, I received a positive."

"I was a Doubting Thomas at first," Lisa smiled, "but when the Corps of Engineers picked the same spot for our pond that Craig had already discerned with the pendulum, I came around. The universe does speak to us, if we'll just listen and ask the right questions."

The brick-lined Chartres labyrinth spread out under our feet, the pond visible through a clearing in the trees, opposite the entrance. Altar stones, as Lisa called them, were arranged in the center, topped with a sphere formed by overlapping metal bands.

"It's a Genesa crystal, a sacred geometric ball," Lisa explained. "It has an energy dynamic all its own that spreads out into the surrounding area and reflects a oneness. The whole interconnectedness piece is what I felt from the beginning when I walked my first labyrinth in Houston. I became aware of people who had walked it before and people who would come after, as well as the people I was passing on the path that evening."

She looked at Craig, hesitated briefly, then faced me. "And I know that what I'm going to say next will really blow your mind ... but I believe our labyrinth is a gateway to our brothers and sisters who are extraterrestrial. One night we were in the labyrinth, open and vulnerable to communication, and I had an experience. It wasn't a visual experience, but a knowing and vibrational experience of communion with an extraterrestrial, an awareness of star nations who have a higher consciousness, vibration and frequency. I believe that our labyrinth is a portal to further heart communication with our star nation brothers and sisters."

Lisa took a deep breath then continued with assurance, "The other element that I feel is important with our particular labyrinth is the connection with the natural evolution through the zodiac—of leaving the domination and warring paradigm of the Piscean age and moving into the Aquarian age of harmony, balance and nurturing."

I thanked Lisa and Craig for their openness as we walked back to the house for a healthy lunch of fresh vegetables from the garden, served on Lisa's grandmother's dishes. I had much to ponder as we continued our conversation and then later that afternoon as I walked their labyrinth alone.

EN ROUTE

Mobile, Alabama
Hotel
May 22, 2013

EARLIER THIS AFTERNOON I stepped into Lisa's labyrinth with an intention to be receptive to new ideas, sensations, to whatever the labyrinth held for me. I was still processing what Lisa had shared about their labyrinth in connection to star nations and the zodiac, as well as assimilating Craig's information about the aquaponics system, rain catchment process and solar panel efficiency.

By the time I had circled for ten minutes or more, my breathing had begun to even out. The frenzy of thoughts gradually eased. I focused my attention on the dirt path at my feet, the pond, trees, guineas … and a pine cone.

I stopped, picked it up, rotated it slowly in my hand. Gray, prickly, like hundreds of others; yet as I scanned the labyrinth, I realized that it was the only pine cone on the path. I resumed my walk along the outer ring, but stopped once again. I started to cry.

Karen Speerstra, the woman whose labyrinth I visited in Vermont a year ago, materialized in my mind, smiling the same smile I remember so fondly. I think of her often, and we email from time-to time. But for some reason, today, I distinctly felt her presence. In a recent email she spoke of the cancer's progression and the hospice care she's receiving in her home.

I knew, without a doubt, that the pine cone was meant for her. I had no idea why. There were no pine cones around Karen's labyrinth. There had been no mention of pine cones as we talked. Perhaps it was something Lisa said about sensing a feminine, nurturing energy in the Middle Earth labyrinth. Karen wrote extensively about the Divine Feminine in her book *Sophia: The Feminine Face of God.*

What I did know was that I would mail it to her. I cupped the pine cone in my hands as I finished the walk.

I showed Lisa the pine cone and shared Karen's story with her before I left. "I love the thought that a pine cone from our labyrinth will keep her company," she said. "It's all about connectedness."

Follow-up
July 28, 2013

Email from Karen:

> "Twylla, your beautiful pine cone arrived on my 73rd birthday. Joel [her son] had just tidied up the labyrinth, so my plan was to walk it later in the afternoon, which I did. I thought I would carry the pine cone to the center and leave it there and then decided—no. I want it close to my computer to remind me of your thoughtfulness, your writing project and your great passion for all that is important in this life. So it's here. Thanks! Many blessings!"

She died four months later.

In her journey toward dying, Karen wrote of my thoughtfulness, my writing, my passion.

The gift of a simple pine cone returned blessings to the giver.

10

Heart in the Heartland

Illinois, Wisconsin, Michigan, Indiana, Ohio

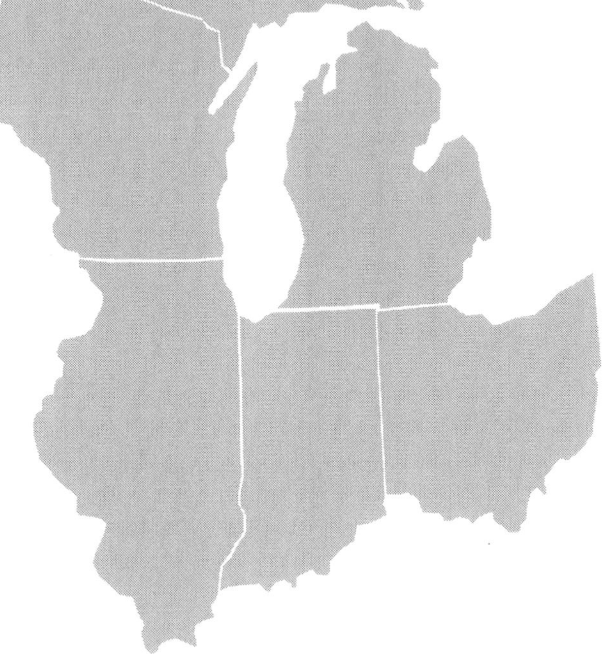

Top, left to right: Susie Silberhorn, Illinois; Dianne Witte, Wisconsin. Middle, left to right: Kathe Thompson, Indiana; Kay Stolsonburg, Michigan. Right: Linda Landis, Ohio.

~ Twylla's journal ~

LaGuardia Airport, NYC
June 22, 2013

THIS IS THE most challenging trip so far, five states—five sizable states—in four days. And today is the most challenging of the four, Illinois and Wisconsin in one day. A two-hour drive north of Chicago, plus another hour and a half across the border to Wisconsin, then retrace my route to a hotel close to Chicago Midway Airport. In comparison, the other three days feel like leisurely summer outings, one day per state, then home.

Susie, Dianne, Kay, Kathe and Linda. Women I only know as names on emails—friendly, inviting emails—are expecting me. I can't wait to meet them!

Susie Silberhorn
Garden Prairie, Illinois
June 22, 2013

I TURNED LEFT at the "Susie's Garden Patch" sign behind a line of five other cars. We caravaned down a gravel road past a house on the right toward a barn, silo and greenhouses to park opposite an open-air building. Fresh produce, including the reddest strawberries I'd ever seen, spilled from baskets and bins.

I approached a woman wearing khaki shorts and a red shirt, answering a man's question about cucumbers. She noticed me at the same time.

"Are you Susie?" I asked.

"I've been expecting you," she answered and without missing a beat turned to her daughter and told her to take over. We climbed the steps to Susie's house where she offered me iced tea or water in my choice of Mason jars.

"So, about my labyrinth," Susie began as I scrambled to push the voice memo button on my iPhone. "Labyrinths just kind of stumbled into my life. I'd never walked one until I built this one here. My husband and I bought this farm, all 82.5 acres of it, in '85 to grow vegetables, strawberries and stuff. Mazes were a big thing around here on Halloween and we thought about building one, but we didn't really like them. Then I read about labyrinths in *Reader's Digest,* and I felt it. My father used to say, 'I got to feel it in my bones.' Same thing for me. You just know. I bought a book about labyrinths, studied it, then needed to pick a spot for one."

She took a breath and continued, "I asked my husband to give me some land for it. I knew I wanted the path to be big enough so two people could pass, about three feet wide. That required a lot of land, about 150 x 150. I think it's a quarter mile in and out. When I do things, it's grandiose! It's all grass, as you'll see. Grass and wildflowers."

Susie waved to customers as we stepped out the back door on the way to the labyrinth. She called several of them by name, and they answered back with a friendly "Hey there!" "How you doin', Susie?" or "Nice to see you."

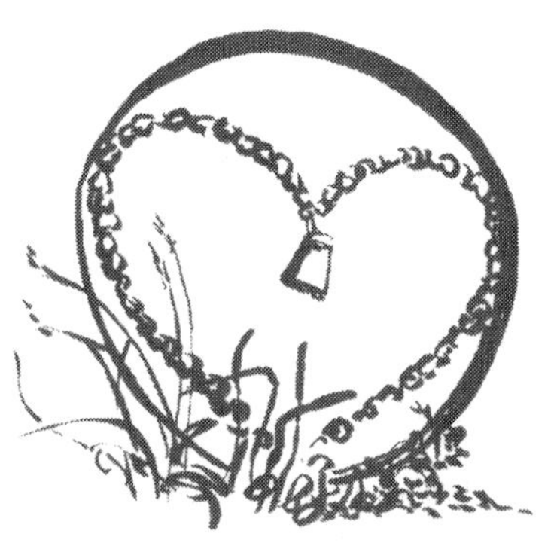

A short walk from the house, Susie abruptly stopped and announced, "Here it is!" Otherwise I would have kept going, unaware that the tall grass I was walking into was actually the labyrinth.

"I told you it's big," she grinned. "It's a walk, for sure. I've actually had people walk in, then cut across and go right to the center. It takes me a while to mow it. I hand mow it about every ten days this time of year. I take my time. I'm pretty picky about my mowing. You'll see that I mow a heart in the center where that cowbell is. I'm carving some eagles and owls to put here at the entrance, and I've got a mushroom that someone gave me to put somewhere in it. I'll know where to put it when I feel it.

"One thing I really want to do bad is put a journal or something out here so if people want to sit and write something, they can. It would be for people to put their feelings in. Once I figure out how to keep it waterproof, I'll get it out here," Susie assured me.

I had no doubt about it.

Sounds of women's voices carried from rows of strawberries as they "picked their own." More cars turned off the highway at Susie's sign. A train whistle sounded in the distance announcing its imminent arrival on the tracks yards away from the labyrinth.

"I named it for my Grandma, Mary. You probably saw her picture on my web thing. Everything she did was from the heart. She asked for nothing and gave and gave and gave. And in the Bible it says you get back ten-fold. Believe me, she got it back. After I finished this labyrinth, I stood here looking at it and I go, 'That's Grandma.' I could feel it."

Susie glanced over the grasses toward the parking lot, "I've got to get back to work, but you walk it as long as you want to. It brings me joy to see people walking it. I can't explain it. Sometimes it almost brings tears to my eyes."

Twenty minutes later, I sat on a bench in the heart-shaped center, across from a heart-shaped metal sculpture adorned by a dangling cowbell. Surrounding me was a labyrinth named for a grandmother who gave from the heart, built by a woman who clearly followed in her footsteps.

* * *

Dianne Witte
Edgerton, Wisconsin
June 22, 2013

DIANNE OPENED THE sliding glass door and pointed beyond the wooden deck, arbor and neatly groomed grass to her backyard labyrinth. I didn't see it. What I did see, though, would have inspired Monet to get out his paintbrush.

"Dianne, these colors are ..." The only words I could think of to fill in the blank seemed trite or grossly inadequate. "Brilliant" was the one I hurriedly settled on as Dianne guided me past the koi pond covered in water lilies into a yard overflowing with flowers.

"My labyrinth started with plants," she said. "I created the original one closer to the house with plantings of marigolds and canna, then it evolved to the larger labyrinth further back. My first memory of a labyrinth was one planted with perennials. I couldn't walk it, though, because it was too deteriorated."

Dianne repositioned a purple clematis vine along the curved arbor as we ducked underneath. "I walked a labyrinth for the first time at Unity church here in Edgerton," she continued. "It was the indoor kind made of canvas. The walk was fine, but the idea of combining the labyrinth with gardening is what really appealed to me.

"I get so distracted by the plants when I enter my labyrinth that I don't even walk it that much," Dianne added. "I end up stopping all the way around to pull weeds. As if on cue, she leaned forward and snipped a suspicious-looking shoot, then straightened up and declared...

"Welcome to my labyrinth!"

We stood gazing at row upon row, or more accurately, circle upon circle of flowers. I searched for the labyrinth's classical design among blossoms that flowed over, shot up, and spread out along its border. Purplish-blue delphinium spiked to the top of my head while mounds of yellow daisies hovered at my feet.

"I've named it the Transformation Labyrinth," Dianne explained, "because you can see the transformation in the flowers. From tulips to lupine in the spring, then delphiniums and lavender, on through day lilies, black-eyed Susans, and echinacea, followed soon by frost, then blankets of winter snow. And I think that people who walk it can be transformed too. That's what the labyrinth's turns represent to me, that we're always changing."

Dianne deadheaded faded blossoms and tossed them aside. "I built it in May, which is under the sign of Taurus. I did some research and found an esoteric astrologer, William Meader, who says that Taurus is the sign most related to the transformation of personal desire into spiritual aspiration.

"This is Archangel Uriel at the entrance. He represents the energy of new beginnings," Dianne said as we stepped onto the path of grass clippings. "You'll find other angels sprinkled about like the guardian angel with her purple dress, and that one over there bent over a row of hollyhocks with her watering can.

"Look at this," she smiled, waving me over to a cracked flowerpot resting on its edge near the labyrinth's center. Mounds of moss, decorated with shiny silver rocks, led to a tiny door-like opening. "If you listen carefully, you'll hear the songs of fairies tending the flowers."

"A fairy house!" I exclaimed. "I've only recently learned about them from my friend Margie, who discovered a forest floor filled with them in Maine.

"Exactly! I became interested in them ..."

Dianne's sentence was cut short when a petite gray bird whizzed past her face and squeezed into the hole of a weathered birdhouse. "Check out the top of the birdhouse and you'll see a goddess," she urged me.

Intrigued by the notion that a goddess lived in Dianne's labyrinth, I eagerly leaned forward to learn her identity, only to discover my own reflection in a mirror.

"Thanks for the compliment," I laughed.

"This labyrinth has brought me so many friendships and now it's brought you. My meditation group was here last week and they were just thrilled. One of the gals said, 'I've never seen anything so gorgeous!' For me, I guess having the labyrinth has become natural, even ordinary. It's just what I'm doing and what the earth and I are working on.

"Like with my flowers and plants," Dianne reflected further, "everything in life is a growing process, evolving. It's like when you walk the labyrinth, you can't get lost. But you can transform."

Dianne sat on a bench opposite the entrance as I took pictures from every angle trying to capture the shape of the labyrinth. Even from a ridge nearby or atop a rickety wheelbarrow, I couldn't see the pattern clearly. The plants were in the way. I lay aside my camera and reframed that thought. The plants *are* the way.

Kay Stolsonburg
Middleville, Michigan
June 23, 2013

MICHIGAN, SWELTERING IN ninety-plus degree temperatures, didn't match the snowy image I had always associated with the state. Yet here was grass, fully leafed out trees, even a non-frozen lake behind Kay's house. I was sweating before I reached her front door.

Kay's sleeveless dress and bare feet were the next clue that I had made a serious wrong turn and ended up in Florida. "You're in the right place," she laughed. "Get cooled off then we'll walk the labyrinth. It's in full sun this time of day."

"I've been working to get it ready for you ever since you called. Grass had really grown over the bricks about a couple of inches. I tried a sod cutter, going around all sides of every brick, but there are 2,400 bricks! So I hired a friend's son, and he finished a couple of days ago. And talk about a difference in energy! I think the labyrinth has been setting things up to get itself cleaned. It's been there for ten years, so it's about time."

Kay's grandchildren ran inside needing water, snacks and blasts of air conditioning. I could relate, both to their requests and Kay's role, with four grandchildren of my own. And like any grandmother, she was an expert at multitasking, so she kept talking.

"A friend once asked me, 'Why do you want your own labyrinth?' "

"So I can walk it every day if I want to," I told her. "One summer I actually did walk it ninety-nine days in a row, but then there are stretches when I don't walk it. When it's covered with snow and I can't see the path, I just start walking, putting in turns here and there until I reach the center. Then I follow my footsteps back out to get the energy flowing. I've even walked it in the dark wearing a headlamp."

Kay refilled my water glass and continued. "I walked three labyrinths before I built mine, two in California, and one close to our house mowed in a churchyard. The night before 9/11, I kept hearing a voice inside me say, 'Go walk the labyrinth. Go walk the labyrinth.' I had not been to that labyrinth at the church before and wasn't exactly sure where it was located, but I found it and walked. All hell broke loose, of course, the next day. I don't know if that walk was preparing me for what was to come, but I do know that I was connected to the labyrinth."

Kay pointed out her front window to a flat piece of land across the street. "I knew our property over there was the only place big enough to build a Chartres labyrinth. But there were all kinds of construction materials on it, plus an old drain field and big brush pile. So we started by burning the brush pile and I accidentally set the neighbor's woods on fire."

She shook her head from side to side, clearly laughing at herself.

"That slowed me down a bit, but fortunately no one got hurt. Let's walk over there so you can picture the whole process."

The labyrinth lay across a manicured piece of lawn that could house at least ten putting greens. It beamed with more than noonday sun, pride perhaps, or an eagerness to be walked.

"Just imagine heavy equipment out here leveling the land, then loads of top soil, an underground sprinkler system, followed by grass," Kay explained. "That all happened in one summer, then the next summer I put in the labyrinth. I had enough space for one that measured sixty feet in diameter, so I converted the forty-two-foot dimensions of the Chartres Cathedral labyrinth to fit the land. The math was the easy part."

Easy for her to say.

"The labor intensive part, of course, was all the measuring, spray painting and digging the trench for each brick—with a big kitchen knife.

Kay moved toward the entrance marked by a planter of amethyst-colored petunias. "I think this whole labyrinth movement is healing the planet, I do. In my own little way I've contributed to that. And walking the labyrinth gives me a sense of what God wants me to do on a here-on-this-planet basis like, 'I'm here. What's next?'

"Now that it's renewed," she reflected, "I have a feeling that more people will come. I put out an invitation on Facebook for a moonlight walk in a couple of days. It's here to be shared.

"Let's walk before we get sunburned," she recommended, waving me to go first.

We slipped off our shoes and eased into the labyrinth's gracious welcome. I felt it the minute the warm Michigan grass touched my feet.

* * *

EN ROUTE

Marion, Indiana
Hotel
June 23, 2013

My cell phone died an hour-and-a half before I reached the hotel this afternoon.

No GPS.

No map in the glove compartment.

No idea how to get from Point A to Point B.

The only logical option was to stop and charge it. But where? A gas station or convenience store seemed a bit dodgy. Starbucks? Dunkin' Donuts? None in sight. I faked my way through Battle Creek until the inevitable wrong turn propelled me into a community of car dealerships, self storage units, truck rental companies, and a friendly looking Sherwin-Williams Paint Store. I parked and went in.

I nonchalantly scoped out the place. One employee, a young guy, explained caulking options to the lone customer. A woman, who appeared even younger, sat at a table beside the paint samples, writing in a loose-leaf notebook.

"I know this is a strange request, but could I charge my phone somewhere in your store?" I asked the young guy after the customer left. I noticed the word *Manager* on his name tag. I filled him in on my story.

"Uh … sure," he said. "There's an outlet behind the counter." He took my phone and plugged it in.

"I'll just hang out for half an hour or so, if that's okay," I said. "My husband has actually been talking about staining our deck this summer," which was almost true. "Do you have some samples?"

Behind me, the young woman spoke, "Hi! There's plenty of room at the table, if you'd like to sit down. My husband can get you a glass of water." She smiled at the manager.

At that moment I had a choice, as we always do when someone offers us a kindness.

I could politely say, "Thanks, but I'll just wander around," or, "Thanks, I'd appreciate some water," and pull up a chair.

For some reason, today, I chose the latter.

No customers came in during the next half hour on a slow Sunday afternoon. The husband joined us at the table and the three of us talked. She frequently kept him company on Sundays, she said, catching up on reading and projects for her graduate degree. They had only been married a couple of years. They spoke of their dreams for the future.

"I just found out that I'm pregnant," she announced. He reached across the table and held her hand.

"Tell us about you," she requested politely.

I shared a synopsis of my journey then showed them a photo of our children and grandchildren. I sipped the cool water.

"My phone must be charged by now, at least enough to get me to the hotel." I got up reluctantly, shook hands with him and hugged her. "Thank you both. I wish you the very best."

In the parking lot, I turned on the air conditioner, leaned back into the seat and waited for the car to cool down.

The gift of a chance encounter.

Connection.

Kindness.

I smiled and drove on up the road.

Kathe Thompson
Indianapolis, Indiana
June 24, 2013

I TURNED ONTO a quiet street lined with established shade trees. Neatly mowed lawns flowed seamlessly from one house to the next. Kathe's gray frame house trimmed in white exuded a calm, tranquil presence. I assumed that the woman who opened the door would reflect a similar demeanor. She did, and something more.

"I find my peace through meditation and movement," Kathe began," as she filled our cups with nettle tea. "That inner peace you can always access through every challenge in life. You can find it in a variety of ways like the labyrinth, yoga and even spinning. As a health coach, I help people on their healing journeys while I continue my own."

The warmth of the tea and mid-morning sun circulated through my body as Kathe and I chatted on her deck. In the middle of the backyard, the labyrinth waited patiently for us to finish.

"And my labyrinth is a way for me to have fun!" Kathe laughed gaily.

"Fun?" I asked, comfortably settled in for a soothing conversation about peace and healing.

"Yes, that's really how this labyrinth got started. A friend told me about a winter solstice labyrinth walk she had attended then loaned me a couple of labyrinth books. I'd never walked one, but it really spoke to me right off the bat. We have a lot of spiritual friends and I said to them, 'Why don't we build a labyrinth and have a winter solstice celebration?

"Twelve people showed up for what we called The Big Build," Kathe shared. "It was a beautiful fall day after Thanksgiving 2006. We made a big pot of chili. A couple of friends created the design by using a pole and string. Everyone else helped spray paint the lines."

Kathe opened a loose-leaf notebook and turned to photos of the day. "My labyrinth notebook," she explained.

"Then came the solstice event the next month. Here's a copy of the invitation." Kathe removed a colorful sheet of paper from the notebook.

> WINTER SOLSTICE CELEBRATION.
> Greetings my spiritual friends!!
> You are invited to a spiritual gathering to start your holiday season.
> BEING PEACEFUL
> while it may be in the midst of chaos

"And here's a copy of the recipe for White Bean, Chicken and Pumpkin Soup that we served. I gave the recipe to five people to prepare so we had plenty. Forty people came!

"I talked about the history of labyrinths," Kathe went on, "and a friend led a guided meditation. People visited, ate, and walked the labyrinth. We built a fire in the pit over there. The labyrinth was lined with paper bag luminaries. The evening was such a wonderful mix of a spiritual event and party."

I imagined the grass labyrinth dressed up for the occasion, adorned in circles of flickering light. But before that picture had time to focus, Kathe added another.

"Oh, then on my birthday one year, I invited friends to walk the labyrinth. It rained, but that didn't stop people from walking it, in bare feet, carrying umbrellas— all colors."

Then another ...

"I've had church groups here, women's groups and a Brownie troop. I've led yoga sessions on it. And now, you're here. When I registered it on the Labyrinth Locator, I never dreamed that someone would call and ask to walk it. I just wanted to be in the energy of the world as someone who has a labyrinth.

"It's not so much that my labyrinth is special, like elaborate or gorgeous, or made out of shrubs," Kathe reflected. "It's the special things we've done with it, the groups and the energy we've brought to it. It's about accessing the peace and balance that already exists within us."

Setting her teacup in its saucer and stepping off the deck, Kathe gestured for me to follow, "Come look at it more closely."

Unruly mounds of grass outlined the seven-circuit path like hair joyfully escaping the stylist's shears. A cherub hugging a bunny waited for us in the center.

"Weeds can be beautiful in their own way," Kathe said as she reached down to gather a handful of grass clippings. "I thought about mulch or pavers, but they just wouldn't feel the same. The grass grows so tall that we mow the whole thing over twice a year then let it grow back. I like the feel of the tall grass, though, especially in the wind. I sweep my hands along it as I walk."

We paused to pat the cherub before circling out.

"It's just a basic grass labyrinth," Kathe smiled. That's all it is."

A basic grass labyrinth, indeed. Permeated with Kathe's balance of peacefulness and fun, it offers a most generous and welcoming spirit to all who enter.

* * *

EN ROUTE

Poem jotted in journal
Somewhere between Indianapolis, Indiana
and Columbus, Ohio
June 24, 2013

Angels!
Angels on earth
Giant
White
Long-legged angels whose
wings spin in the wind.
O'er
silver silos
rusted tractors
rows of
greening crops
they hover
with
graceful energy.
Whoosh
Whoosh
Whoosh
Until the air stills
and
they slow
to
silence.
I stand
Mesmerized.

◊◊◊

Linda Landis
Baltimore, Ohio
June 25, 2013

I PARKED IN Linda's driveway under a green canopy of interwoven branches. The house lay to the right. Cornfields, as far as the eye could see, stretched to the left. At 8:30 in the morning, the still, cool air felt like the calm before a busy day. A door slammed and Linda's voice rang out, "Twylla, you're here!" We hugged like old friends.

The story that Linda told me, within ten minutes of our greeting, was not one I would have dreamed possible from the woman sitting opposite me on her porch. She smiled, laughed, was incredibly warm and friendly. She seemed at peace.

"I do have to tell you, before you hear about my labyrinth, what happened in my life. Our son was killed in an automobile accident."

Tears gathered. I leaned forward and touched her hand, one mother to another.

"That was the greatest challenge in my life, but it was also the greatest opportunity," Linda went on. "That's when I really started meditating, and that's when I got more into my spiritual life. I had planned to create a meditation garden, but then I read about labyrinths. Once I did, I was totally connected. I knew I would build one. I just knew it. But then the accident happened."

I listened.

"After that, I just couldn't get it done. I tried. I even had a huge dump truck load of sand delivered to place the stones in, but the pile just sat there. I needed to do a lot of internal work. My internal landscape was changing and had to change before I could put the labyrinth in the ground.

"Also during that period of time," she continued, "I had a heart attack. This is all from the broken heart. My health wasn't good for a while, so that was another reason the labyrinth was delayed. Things don't happen overnight. You're changing and these are things that are for your good. So you do change. The labyrinth out there is a part of the change."

Linda pointed in the direction of the labyrinth, but from where we sat, I could see only a clearing completely sheltered by shade trees. The heads of orange day lilies peeked around large rocks. Dense rows of corn formed the far border.

"When I felt the time was right to put the labyrinth in, I did it all in one day, by myself. The labyrinth had been in my head all those years and then I finally built it. It was totally liberating! I just went out there with a piece of rebar, a rope and a can of spray paint. I measured out the lines, sprayed them, then lay the rocks down. All the rocks came from our yard. I feel like they were waiting for me. My husband will tell you that one of my favorite things to do is move rocks around. When he came home that afternoon and saw the labyrinth, he couldn't believe it. He probably thought, 'She's never gonna do that.' "

Linda laughed with a brightness that warmed my spirit.

"This is my sacred space," Linda said, as we entered the clearing. "And I'm so grateful to have it. I usually walk in the morning. It faces east so it feels like I'm taking on the new day. I've walked it so many times, I could probably walk it blindfolded. It helps me realize that even when I seem to be far away from the center, or my goals, I'm always moving closer. Then the next thing I know, I'm right where I'm supposed to be."

We walked to the center together, stepping over and around items of significance to Linda. Fragments of a blue plate, pieces of glass bottles and a cracked tile decorated with two raised dragonflies.

"Things I found in the cornfield," Linda explained. "People throw things in there and I find them. The shells came from the beach, a place I really like to go."

She sat on the large rectangular stone in the center. "This is the only part of the labyrinth I needed help with. A nice man with a front loader put it in place the very day I called him.

"Last year, I realized that I was ready to share my labyrinth with others," Linda reflected, "so I put it on the Labyrinth Locator. Before then I felt very private about it. It's still my space, but my heart had grown enough so I could open it up to other people."

Her heart had grown. The heart which had once been broken.

Breeze drifted from the cornfield through the trio of wind chimes, into sacred space.

11

On the Heels of Laura Ingalls Wilder

Minnesota, North Dakota, South Dakota, Iowa

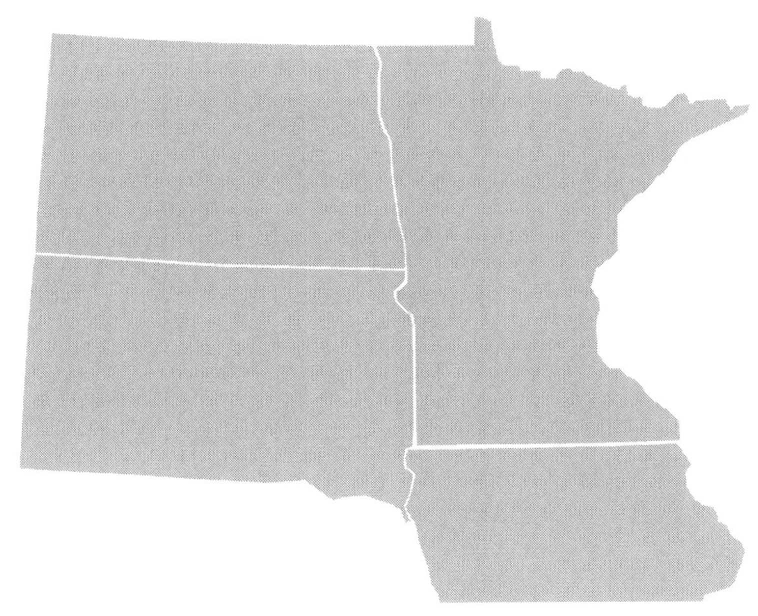

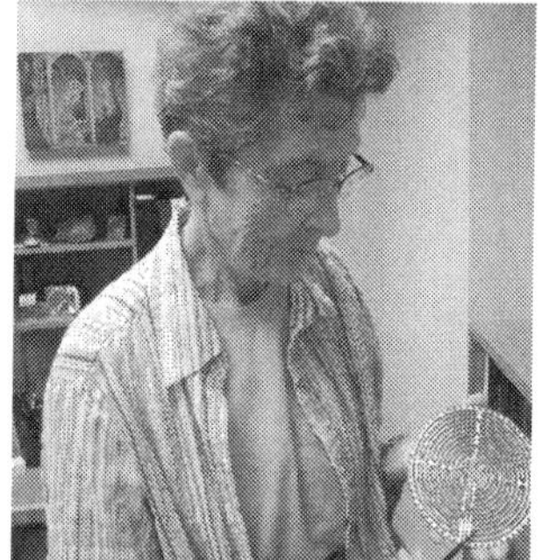

Top, left to right: Mary Drier, Iowa; Kate Raatz, Minnesota. Bottom, left to right: Sister Gemma Peters, North Dakota ; Jeannie Ammon and Carol Baum, South Dakota.

~ Twylla's journal ~

On a flight from Newark, New Jersey
to Minneapolis, Minnesota
August 27, 2013

Tomorrow afternoon—thirty-six hours and 1,450 miles from now—I'll be in DeSmet, South Dakota. I will have already visited women and walked labyrinths in Minneapolis and Bismarck, North Dakota and will be driving toward Dell Rapids, South Dakota. My stop in DeSmet has nothing to do with labyrinths. It's a detour of thirty miles to stand on a prairie, the same prairie where Laura Ingalls Wilder stood as a young girl in the 1880s.

I grew up reading *Little House on the Prairie* books, picturing Laura's braids and calico dresses, Pa playing the fiddle and Ma churning butter. As an adult, I know that the stories are romanticized versions of dangerous covered wagon journeys and rugged homestead life. But as a child, they touched my heart and enchanted me as a reader. They still do.

I want to gaze across miles of golden prairie and imagine myself as Laura, running with joyful abandon through waist-deep grass. I want to snip a sprig of prairie grass and press it in my copy of *By the Shores of Silver Lake*, one of Laura's four books set in DeSmet.

I'm traveling on my own again, at least no one will physically be sitting in the car beside me. A diverse group of women's voices from *The Help* by Kathryn Stockett will accompany me. They began telling their stories two months ago on highways crisscrossing Illinois, Wisconsin, Michigan, Indiana and Ohio. With each advancing chapter, their voices grow stronger, more determined.

I'll be in good company.

* * *

Kate Raatz
Elk River, Minnesota
August, 27, 2013

IF MICHIGAN FELT hot to me in June, Minnesota was ablaze in August, literally, with forest fires burning in large areas of the state.

"Day twenty without rain and a high of ninety-six," the announcer blasted over the car radio. As I parked in Kate's driveway and walked toward the front door, I noticed that the field in front of her house looked parched. The field, I would soon learn, contained her labyrinth.

A bench opposite the entrance to the labyrinth caught the fringe of early afternoon shade. "Let's talk here," Kate suggested. "It's a cooler spot even in this heat." We brushed acorns onto ground already littered with them. "They're everywhere. It's a sign of a bad winter coming."

I wondered what the signs had been for summer.

"The labyrinth's only been here a year. *We've* only been here a year," Kate clarified. "When we were looking for a house, one of my criteria was that there had to be room for a labyrinth. There was never a question about it. And, as you can see, it's a big one—140 feet across."

If I stood on the bench, I could see the far edge. But seated, the grass path beyond the center faded into waves of endless sunshine.

"Before I walked a labyrinth, I had been searching in the areas of spirituality and faith. I call it more of a *dis*-rest than *un*-rest," Kate explained. "I wasn't happy being Lutheran; it just didn't fit me well. I met some members of a pagan community and one of the ladies had a labyrinth. I walked it, my first one, in 2008.

Wiping her forehead with a tissue, she went on, "I learned about the positive effects of meditation and knew I should be doing it. But I can't sit still and meditate. I have to be moving, so I needed a tool. When I learned about the labyrinth, it was like 'Yep! I've got to have one.' It took me until last year to find a place.

"Stand here by these rocks and you can see how we laid it out," she suggested.

Two large, gray stones jutted out of the ground at the entrance. Lines of smaller rocks edged both sides of the path like lights on a runway, then appeared only sporadically throughout the rest of the labyrinth.

"These two stones came from land I grew up on near Detroit Lakes, Minnesota," Kate said as she touched the peak of the stone nearest her. "One day I'll have the whole thing lined with rocks. It'll take me years and trips to places."

I recognized the eagerness in Kate's voice, that familiar hint of anticipation for a journey that lay out there—somewhere.

"When I got ready to build it, my intuition told me where to put the center so my husband started in that spot with a tractor/tiller machine. I carried a diagram of the seven-circuit labyrinth and walked where the path should go. He followed me. We veered to the right a lot and had to start over. If we did it again, the process would be smoother. But it's fine.

"You can probably tell that the center is larger than the standard dimensions," Kate pointed out. "That's because I have a vision of adding a medicine wheel at some time."

Kate walked backwards into the labyrinth, maintaining eye contact with me, until we both reached the first turn and stopped. "Labyrinths have been around forever, you know, and they have a power just in being what they are. This one has only been here for a year, but it's strong already. It gets a little stronger every time I share it. It's a love thing, I think. Like it becomes more itself every time it's shared, every time it helps someone. I hadn't put that in words before, but I like it."

Further along the path we reached an island of multi-colored blooms, which had somehow survived amidst a sea of yellow and brown grass.

"Cosmos," Kate named them. "Sometimes I come out and mess with the plants more than walk, and even that's a meditation. It calms me. Somehow it just makes all my anxiety not matter. Not that I'm a terribly anxious person, but it's like a reset button."

I recalled my arrival when *parched* was the only, and obvious, word I could choose to describe Kate's labyrinth. Yet in the hour she and I had talked, Kate had not mentioned that word once. Instead, she spoke of her labyrinth's power, strength, of its love and calm presence.

The difference? Another word. *Relationship.*

EN ROUTE

I-94 between Fargo and Bismark, North Dakota
Notes scribbled on a gas receipt
August 28, 2013

SUNFLOWERS! THOUSANDS and THOUSANDS—probably MILLIONS—of sunflowers! Who knew there were sunflowers in North Dakota? Yellow in every direction.

Their heads tower above mine, stretching to grasp every ounce of sunshine. Van Gogh wouldn't know where to start.

I'll just pull off the road and sit here beside them for a while.

Sister Gemma Peters
Benedictine Sisters of Annunciation Monastery
Bismarck, North Dakota
August 28, 2013

"If you are coming all the way to North Dakota, I'll be glad to share the story of our labyrinth," Sister Gemma wrote in response to my email. "Let's meet in the morning."

I tore myself away from the fields of sunflowers so I would arrive at the monastery by 10:30. Sister Gemma welcomed me and pointed the way down a long, sloping sidewalk toward the flattest piece of flat land I had even seen.

"This labyrinth is in such a peaceful place, like the first labyrinth I walked at a retreat center years ago," Sister Gemma commented as we walked side by side toward the labyrinth. "When I returned home, I said to the sisters, 'I think having a labyrinth would be another way to touch people's lives, to help them hear God amidst the beauty of nature.' "

A mowed path connected the sidewalk to the labyrinth where a solitary tree stood in the center of eleven concentric circles of rocks. Beyond that—prairie—broken only by a lagoon glistening in the distance.

"We've had the hardest time with that ash tree," Sister Gemma explained. "Every year I'd wrap the trunk to keep the deer from chewing it, but then it got too big and hard to wrap. So I finally said, 'God, you must want a plain walk so everyone can see it.' "

"The labyrinth's been here for ten years now. It's aged and has its own character. I still come down here sometimes to center myself. I ponder how God has blessed me during my sixty-two years as a Benedictine nun.

"I put pamphlets about the labyrinth in here," said Sister Gemma, opening the door to a wooden box nailed to a tall pole. "They explain what a labyrinth is and give people suggestions on how to walk it.

When we built the labyrinth, it was new to people. We had to do some educating."

Sister Gemma's eyes swept the horizon as she slowly rotated her head from left to right, across land and time. "All this was just a field back then," she reflected. "We organized a committee to research and plan the labyrinth and walked all around this area to see where would be a good space. We didn't want it to be too close to the monastery so people could walk in private, without feeling like they were being seen or watched. I mapped it out with my friend Linda Stewart. We based it on the Chartres design, the Christian one.

"Most of the rocks that line it came from the prairie, but there are some that came from all over, even Alaska and Florida. We put out the word that we needed plain rocks with no names or painting on them, nothing to distract people as they walk. We had Boy Scout troops and all kinds of different people help us place them. Some people call it a rock walk, others a reflective walk. I say a prayer walk. It's whatever people need.

"We're people of the prairie," Sister Gemma smiled. "Very earthy. We wanted to walk on the ground. We didn't want a high maintenance labyrinth. It's basic to the prairie."

The sun was almost directly overhead. Sister Gemma shielded her eyes with a hand as she added final details to the story. "When we completed the labyrinth, we blessed it. During the prayer ritual, two bald eagles flew over. They're a sacred sign to Native Americans and that was a sign for us that the labyrinth was truly blessed.

"This time of year I sometimes see people walking it in the evening. You can hear birds sing and coyotes howl out there in the distance. It's the space. Our society needs space to get away from the hectic world.

"I just try to keep the labyrinth uncluttered," she said simply.

"You walk and when you are finished, I will give you a tour of the monastery," Sister Gemma offered as she started the gradual climb back up the sidewalk. "Enjoy your prairie walk."

Within the vastness of a prairie, I stepped into a familiar design. Uncluttered space swelled in every direction. I circled toward the ash tree and breathed, deeply.

EN ROUTE

DeSmet, South Dakota
Hotel
August 28, 2013

I DROVE SIX hours straight from Bismarck to Desmet to arrive at Laura's Living Prairie before sunset, and I made it with one hour to spare! The visitor center had closed at 5:00, but the prairie was wide open. The only visible sign of life, except me, was a rooster pecking beside a replica of Pa's Hayroof Barn. Somewhere in the distance, crickets warmed up for the evening's serenade.

Parking under five enormous trees at the base of a hill, I read the nearby sign:

> Homestead Memorial Site 1880–1887
> Five towering cottonwood trees still stand on the one acre of Pa's original homestead claim.

CHARLES INGALLS PLANTED trees, one each for his wife and daughters, Mary, Laura, Carrie, and Grace. I touched each of the trees' massive trunks in turn and felt the presence of the family they honored.

I climbed the well-traveled path towards a rock marker that designated the spot where the family had lived in a one-room shanty. It was here, the inscription continued "where Ma made a home for the family." As a mother, I instinctively placed myself in Caroline Ingalls shoes—her dirty, well-worn shoes that rarely rested.

The sun slumped behind me as I sat on a lone bench overlooking the prairie. A white-steepled church, cornfields, a smattering of houses, a few trees and a windmill lay in the distance. But mostly grass, miles and miles of grass, stretched to the horizon.

I opened *By the Shores of Silver Lake* and read lines I have marked:

> "It was enormous stillness that made you feel still. And when you were still, you could feel great stillness coming closer. All the little sounds of the blowing grasses and of the horses munching ... and even the sounds of eating and talking could not touch the enormous silence of the prairie."

A warm evening breeze brushed prairie grasses against my legs. I bent over, plucked two stems and secured them snugly between pages of my book.

At the end of this day, I sat in stillness, in "the enormous silence of the prairie."

Jeannie Ammon and Carol Baum
Dell Rapids, South Dakota
August 29, 2013

I DROVE UNDER the arched Dell Rapids Cemetery sign, past headstones on both sides on the narrow gravel road, towards a cornfield in the distance. Two women smiled and waved beside a mailbox painted with black-eyed Susans and butterflies.

"We love to share this garden with others," Jeannie said, leading me under the Mothers' Healing Garden sign into a space overflowing with lush greenery and flowers. "We tell people, 'You just need to come; you need to experience it.' And when they do, they are amazed and we don't have to say another word."

"But we'll tell you all about it," Carol laughed.

Laughter. I didn't expect laughter.

Jeannie's email reply to my request for a visit was heartbreaking. "Our garden and labyrinth have a very important story. Both Carol and I have lost our sons. The labyrinth was born out of grief. It would be our pleasure to share our story with you."

"I always wanted to build a labyrinth in my yard, I guess because my mother had such a love for them," Carol began. "But it wasn't until Jeannie's son, Wyatt, died that I wanted to find a project that we could work on together, to help her through her grief. Our son, Jeremy, had died six years before and projects helped me. I just called her out of the blue one day."

Jeannie stopped in front of a granite bench with Wyatt's name on it. "I remember that day," she said. "I was driving Highway 115. Carol called and said, 'I don't know if you're going to want to do this or not, but I want to build a labyrinth and I want you to help me."

"Before that, we had been talking about how hard it was coming to the cemetery and sitting by a grave, thinking about our sons in the ground," Carol continued. "We had the inspiration to build the labyrinth in the cemetery rather than in one of our yards or a park."

"But we didn't have money for it, and we didn't know if the cemetery board would give us any land," Jeannie added. "All we could do was try. We asked our friend, Nathan, to draw a seven-circuit labyrinth design and we presented it to the board. No graves had been allotted to this space at the time, so they decided to give us this spot where the labyrinth is now—about 35 x 35. Just what we needed.

"That was in 2006. Since then, as you can see, the garden has grown past the labyrinth. The board gave us two more 35 x 35 plots for our open-air chapel, rock wall, and the Sacred Path Scatter Garden."

"Oh look, check out the dragonflies above the corn!" Carol exclaimed.

I turned to see hundreds of dragonflies—flitting, hovering, landing—in bursts of energy so fast it was impossible to single out one.

"There's a legend that the dragonfly is connected to the afterlife," Jeannie said. "When we see them out here, it's like a message that our sons are still with us.

"For me, this garden is a metamorphosis from death to life," she went on."You'll never get over the grief of losing your child, but the pain and sorrow can transform into something that is full of life."

"I come here almost every day," Carol said, sitting down on Jeremy's bench. "If this garden wasn't here, I'd probably never come to the cemetery. And this space has become contagious, in a good way. So many other people love it too and find comfort here. They take care of the flowers, add rocks, just come here and sit."

We followed memorial pavers, engraved with the names of loved ones, to the labyrinth's entrance. A curbed cement edging guided us along a cushioned path of mulch and pine needles.

"About three or four years into my grief process," Jeannie shared as she reached the outer ring, "I was walking the labyrinth, and I seriously didn't think I would feel happy about life again. I got a message, from beyond me somewhere, that said, 'Yes, you will experience joy again.' "

Carol spoke from behind me, "I'm more spiritual than I ever was, not religious. I dropped organized religion, but I never gave up God. I walk the labyrinth the most when I have some speaking to do. I come here and pray that the Holy Spirit helps me through."

A gentle breeze tousled orange zinnias and pink geraniums on its way to the labyrinth. It carried the rhythmic whir of wings, barely audible to someone who wasn't listening. But the two mothers walking the path with me, turned and smiled.

* * *

Mary Dreier
Hubbard, Iowa
August 30, 2013

I'M SLEEPING IN a chicken coop—albeit a fancy one—but a chicken coop, none the less. All the regulars have long since flown the coop. Or maybe they just didn't recognize the place with its frilly curtains, cushy beds and hardwood floors.

"It's where participants stay when they attend my Soul of the Prairie retreats," Mary had said when I asked to visit her labyrinth. "You're welcome to stay. That way, you can get up early and walk the labyrinth at sunrise." I couldn't say yes fast enough.

"Set your alarm for 5:45," Mary said when I arrived. "That will give you plenty of time to get to the center of the labyrinth by sunrise, then walk out and meet me at the peace pole by 7:00. Here's a flashlight but the sun comes up around 6:30, so you won't need it for long. Oh, and no need to lock the door. We're in the country."

Comforting.

At 6:00 a.m., I aimed the flashlight at the peace pole, then the labyrinth's entrance directly beyond. The path disappeared into prairie grass as tall as my shoulders. As I inched forward, I remembered the story Mary had emailed me the week before, the story of how her first labyrinth came to be:

> "This is the farm I moved to thirty years ago when I married my husband. In the midst of raising a family and growing into myself, I felt confined by all that being a family farm wife entails. That is, until one day when I traipsed out to our reconstructed prairie with a measuring tape and lawn mower. With these simple tools and the help of an astonished husband, I created a labyrinth. ... And with this startling act, the land was consecrated. It became more than Iowa farm land. It became a place where land and prayer are one."

I pictured Mary courageously fashioning her first prairie labyrinth, akin to the one I traced with the flashlight's beam. Steps from the center, I clicked off the light to observe a similarly startling act of transformation: black to purple, gray to yellow, hazy to clear. In all directions, the land awakened.

My phone dinged at 6:45. I reluctantly turned my back on prairie vistas and ran back up the path. Mary was waiting for me.

"Let's visit in my office. It was once a coal storage building for a neighborhood one-room schoolhouse. We renovated it to fit a couple of chairs and my desk. Here, you can sit in my great aunt's sewing chair."

Mary gestured toward three windows that faced the labyrinth. "The Soul of the Prairie isn't my only labyrinth," she said. "I have two more, a Chartres in our front yard and a spiral I named the Dancing Spiral. But I like this one best. To me, it's much more free-flowing. I love the rhythm of it. It takes me into a different space. But people have walked the Chartres and gotten into its rhythm and turns. One woman said that it's like walking poetry. I love that!

"Of course, it's a different experience for everyone," she continued, "and I think that labyrinths speak a different language than you and I are speaking now. The labyrinth holds me in my journey and allows me to go deeper into my own story. I can let go. It's like my heart opens."

Mary rested comfortably in her grandmother's rocker. Rectangles of sunlight crept across the floor and touched our feet. A tractor cleared its throat, revved into a high pitch, then settled down to the day's work.

"So much of Soul of the Prairie has come about because of intuition and gut feeling," Mary shared. "It just sort of happened because it needed to happen. I think the world needs places like this, especially in central Iowa where we're all about square fields and straight roads.

"For years I was very, very busy here. I led retreats, individual and group, and facilitated labyrinth walks. I've been a spiritual director and companion to many. Some on-going church groups still meet here and hospice workers are coming next week. But now, my energy's flowing toward our new place in northwestern Iowa. After thirty-six years here, Gordon and I are selling the farm.

"I want someone to buy it who honors the earth and wants to keep it open for others to come," Mary smiled.

I had already built the scenario. I could take over Mary's work and Drew could work the land. I wondered what he'd say if I called.

"So, want to buy a farm in Iowa? It comes with three labyrinths and a tractor. Oh, and a chicken coop!"

12

In the Company of Friends

Washington, Alaska, Montana, Idaho

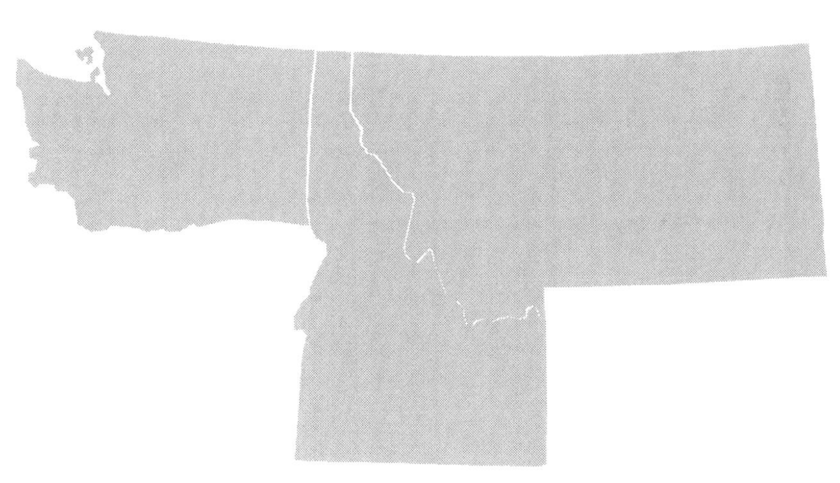

Top row, left to right: Tricia Layden, Washington; Patty Meyer, Montana. Bottom row, left to right: Rebecca Foster, Idaho; Janis Burns Buyarski, Alaska.

~ Twylla's journal ~

Atlanta airport (layover from NYC to Seattle)
September 17, 2013

> "A labyrinth is like an old friend. Like old friends, you return to it again and again."
>
> ~Karen Speerstra (Vermont)

I UNPINNED THIS quote from my bulletin board last night and tucked it in my journal. It sums up the next eleven days in one sentence. This trip is all about returning to a labyrinth and to friends.

The labyrinth—the Merciful Love Labyrinth in Juneau, Alaska, the first I ever walked over a decade ago.

The friends—Juneau friends. Women I've known longer than I've known the labyrinth. Women with whom I taught school, raised children, hiked trails, endured rain, and applauded sunlight.

VIVIAN (NOW IN SEATTLE) will meet me at the Seattle airport this afternoon and drive me to Tricia Layden's labyrinth during my five-hour layover. She'll drop me off later for my flight to Juneau, where I will facilitate two labyrinth retreats.

Margie will pick me up at the Juneau airport and host me.

Geri will return me to the airport on the twenty-third.

Seventeen friends will attend the labyrinth retreat I'm facilitating on the twentieth at the Shrine of St. Therese. Eighteen more, including some new faces, will attend the second retreat on the twenty-first.

Mary (now in Sagle, Idaho) will drive with me to labyrinths in Montana and Idaho.

Vivian will host me for a night on my return trip through Seattle.

Circling back,
I am encircled
by friends.

* * *

Tricia Layden
SeaTac, Washington
September 17, 2013

On one hand, 2,800 miles (New York City to Seattle) is the longest distance I've traveled in one day to visit a labyrinth. On the other, 1.5 miles (SeaTac airport to Tricia's house) is the shortest.

With only minutes to reminisce after Vivian picked me up at the airport, we promptly arrived at Tricia's house. She was waiting for us at the top of her driveway.

"About a month ago, another person who had a layover at the airport came by and walked my labyrinth," Tricia said as she guided us up the steps to the door. Another time, I drove up the driveway and found several people walking it. But that's why I put it on the Labyrinth Locator. It's always open.

"You can get a good view of it here at the kitchen table. Have a seat and I'll make us some tea. And you can start looking through my picture album. I tried to document the whole process of building it."

Glancing over the blue bottles on the windowsill, Vivian and I saw the seven-circuit labyrinth below, sheltered on its far side by towering evergreens. Street traffic and neighbors' houses were completely hidden, providing the labyrinth and its walkers a more private setting.

"We first had to rototill the ground, then I roped my women's spirituality group into helping me rake the rocks and clumps of dirt. This is what it looked like then," she said, turning to a photo at the beginning of the book. "I was trying to figure out the right measurements when my son finally said, 'Mom, just get out of the way and I'll help you with it.' He figured out the math, put in stakes and string, the whole thing."

"This is fascinating!" Vivian said. "I had no idea, before Twylla told me, that people build labyrinths in their yards. How did you even know you wanted one?"

"I walked my first one at a Crones Counsel meeting."

"Crones?" I interrupted, picturing stoop-shouldered old women in fairy tales. Hansel and Gretel came to mind.

"We adopted that name on purpose as a way to reclaim it, like wise women of ancient cultures."

"Ohhh," I nodded. I liked the sound of that.

"That first walk really affected me," Tricia went on. "It was so meditative. Then I walked a wild labyrinth, just grass and rocks, right by the ocean in Ireland. I thought, 'I could do this, maybe.' I came home and kept talking about building one until finally a friend said, 'Stop talking and do it. If you're going to do it, let's do it!' "

"Here's a picture of my spirituality group at the dedication. We walked to the center and said prayers. One of the best parts of building it was doing it with other women."

I smiled at the photo—women in the center of a labyrinth blowing bubbles.

"Let's go on down there, but first take a look at this picture," Tricia said. "You see these tiny plants? One thing I love about them is how they just decided what they wanted to do. I was never a gardener before I put in the labyrinth and we've lived in this house for forty-six years. But now I'm fascinated with my garden. It's special to me."

Tricia brought her hands to her heart and said, "*Namaste,*" as the three of us stood under the wooden arbor facing the labyrinth's entrance. "I give the Spirit of the Labyrinth a *namaste* when I enter and exit and stand in the center. She hasn't told me her name and I don't tell her what she has to be. But I think that because I love the labyrinth, maintain it, and that so many people have walked it, it's really powerful.

"When I walk into the labyrinth, it's like I'm in a different place," Tricia continued. "I open myself to the universe, to the spirit that's here. I'm in my spiritual center."

Thyme, rosemary and sage released their fresh scents as we brushed past on our way around the path. Tricia ran her fingers along lavender stems, held them to her nose and inhaled.

"I tell the plants how much I love them and how beautiful they are. I really believe that everything has energy. I send my good energy to the labyrinth and I get good energy back."

Before she turned to exit the center, Tricia whispered something. At first, I thought she was speaking to Vivian and me but then quickly pieced the words together.

"Thank you for giving us a lovely walk." She was talking, of course, to the labyrinth.

Janis Burns Buyarski
Juneau, Alaska
September 19, 2013

AT THE BEGINNING of this fifty-state journey, I assumed that the Merciful Love Labyrinth at the Shrine of St. Therese in Juneau would not fit my criteria. I assumed it had been envisioned and built by the faceless Catholic Diocese of Juneau, not by a woman. But I would count it anyway! After all, it was my first and favorite. Oh, the assumptions we make.

Margie and I slipped off our shoes and hung our dripping rain jackets on hooks before climbing the stairs to Janis' living room.

"Margie tells me you want to hear the story of the Merciful Love Labyrinth," Janis smiled as we settled in chairs around the coffee table. "Well, that labyrinth and mine are kind of tied together, so I can tell you both stories."

"Wait!" I exclaimed, "You have your own labyrinth? Here?"

"Yes, right outside that window," she pointed. "I built it in 2003, two years after we built the one at the Shrine."

I recaptured enough composure to press the Start button on my phone, then leaned back into my good fortune and listened.

"The labyrinth at the Shrine didn't start as a labyrinth. It started as a meditation garden, or at least that was on the master facility plan. I was on the Shrine Board then and started praying about what we were supposed to do with the garden. During Advent 2000, I attended a weekend retreat at The Center for Contemplation and Action in Albuquerque, where Father Richard Rohr had built a seven-circuit labyrinth.

"My first night there, I kept hearing, 'Go walk the labyrinth. Go walk the labyrinth.' So I did. And all of a sudden, it was like I'd come out of this dry prayer spell. Over the next three days, the labyrinth became a constant companion. Before I left, Father Richard Rohr, himself, shared some of his books about labyrinths with me.

"About six weeks later," Janis continued, "I went to Grace Cathedral and attended Labyrinth Facilitator Training. When I returned, the Shrine Board was still talking about the meditation garden. Then it just came to me. The meditation garden should be a labyrinth. It was winter so my husband, Ed, and I shoveled both a classical and Chartres labyrinth in the snow for the board members to walk."

Janis leaned forward and began talking faster. "Here's the amazing part ... our bishop then, Bishop Warfel, had just attended a meeting in Chicago where he had heard about labyrinths being used in churches. He listened to my idea and said, 'That makes perfect sense to me.' So the decision was made quickly.

"It had to be the divine hand of God!" Janis declared.

"That June we started building it. I'd never been trained in how to build a labyrinth, but somehow Father Thomas Weise and I figured it out. Once we painted the circles, we were ready for people to help place the rocks. More than a hundred volunteers, using wagons and buckets, hauled rocks from the beach and lined the path with them."

Margie and I sat spellbound, unaware for a moment that Janis had stopped speaking, the significance of her story still sinking in. The labyrinth that both of us held so dear, that scores of other walkers cherished, had been inspired by a woman. This woman.

"Thank you, Janis, for your gift of the labyrinth," I said with a deeper sense of gratitude than the simple words expressed.

"I'm a firm believer in God," she said, "and that God creates opportunities for us.

"Now, do you want to hear about my labyrinth?" she laughed. It's much less complicated."

"Please!" I entreated, like a child begging to hear one more chapter before bedtime.

"Well, like I said before, we built it two years later. First we needed to enlarge the drain field and let the soil settle over the winter. Friends came in the summer and helped us spray paint the lines and put rocks on them. It's a nine-circuit modified Chartres, rather than an eleven. When it was completed, Father Thomas blessed it.

"I wanted a labyrinth I could walk whenever I needed like when I came home from a stressful day. And when our two teenage children were dawdling in the morning before school, I'd walk it. It kept me focused and from nagging them too much. Sometimes, I walk it out of gratitude.

"It's pretty soggy out there today, but we can take a look," Janis offered.

After reapplying shoes and jackets, Margie and I waited at the labyrinth's edge as Janis positioned herself in the center for a photo.

From beneath her blue umbrella, she shouted. "I named it Living Waters."

"Perfect!" we yelled back over the sound of pouring rain.

* * *

EN ROUTE

SeaTac Airport (Seattle)
September 23, 2013
"Women Walking"
(poem reflecting on labyrinth retreats)

For two days, I listened to women's footsteps, circling.
A steady rhythm of feet
never faltering,
rarely resting.
I closed my eyes and felt
the constancy of women
walking through the ages.
Constantly present
for others.
Footsteps.

For two days, I listened to women's voices, sharing.
Seekers of Self, they spoke
their truths
from a deep place of knowing.
I leaned forward and heard
the boldness of women
speaking into their own presence.
Boldly claiming the present
for themselves.
Voices.

Patty Meyer
Victor, Montana
September 24, 2013

MARY [LONG-TIME JUNEAU friend who moved to Idaho with her husband, Doug]: "I've love to go with you on a labyrinth trip when you visit our part of the country."

Twylla [woman on a journey, grateful for friends who like to travel]: "Sure! I'd love to have you join me."

A year later. In front of the Redsun Labyrinth sign, Montana.

Mary: "Can you believe we're actually here? This is so amazing!"

Twylla: "It gets more amazing all the time."

PATTY AND HER husband, Helmut, strolled from their house to the parking area below to welcome us. I noted that she stepped gingerly and that he occasionally reached over to lend her his elbow.

"Hi! Thanks so much for taking the time to visit with us," I said.

"I'm glad I was strong enough for your visit. Let's go in here and sit while I tell you about my labyrinth," Patty suggested, pointing to a converted garage.

"I held labyrinth retreats in this building," she explained, once we were all seated beside a classical labyrinth painted on the floor. "My big Chartres labyrinth is up the path from where you parked. It's actually the first labyrinth I ever walked."

Patty shifted positions and continued, "I heard about labyrinths through a friend back in '97 and started researching them, but there wasn't much information. Once I saw the Chartres pattern, I knew I wanted to build one of my own. I can't tell you exactly why. I was a failed sitting meditator so I thought, 'Give my body something to do, and maybe my brain will behave.' "

She laughed quietly.

"But since I was diagnosed with breast cancer—inflammatory,

triple negative—a year ago, it's become a place of healing. Now when I walk into the labyrinth, I release the negativity, fear, pain, worry, everything I'm afraid of."

Patty had written of her breast cancer during our email exchanges. She mentioned that she had completed the latest round of chemotherapy in June.

"Let's walk up there," she said. "I want you to see it."

Mary and I followed the couple along a tree-lined trail edged with logs displaying some of Patty's favorite quotes, one of which we shared:

> *"Tell me, what is it you plan to do with your one wild and precious life?"*
>
> *– Mary Oliver, "The Summer Day"*

Patty paused at the second of three gates and pointed above to tree limbs fashioned into an arch. "This arch is my tribute to Andy Goldsworthy," she noted.

A short distance ahead, Helmut unlatched the final gate to reveal the labyrinth's rings spreading out before us like ever-expanding ripples in a pond.

"It's 108 feet!" he announced. "In and out is about four-fifths of a mile. It took almost twenty-five tons of field stones to line the path."

"I wanted a labyrinth big enough so lots of people could walk it," Patty smiled.

She motioned for Mary and me to cut across the gravel path with her to the center.

"Some people omit the six petals in the middle when they build a Chartres design, but I wanted them. I know they have a Christian meaning, but I read that they also represent the kingdoms of creation. You'll notice that there's a sign in each petal to identify the kingdoms: Mineral, Plant, Animal, Human, Divine and Angelic."

"I stand before each sign and ask the same question," Patty explained. 'What do you have for me?' I receive a different message from each one.

Mineral gives me strength
Plant—tenacity
Animal—unconditional love
Human— support, friendship and love
Divine—healing

And … Angelic reassures me, 'It's not your time. Your body knows what to do.' "

Patty pulled her hood over her head as a misty rain began to fall. "I've been measuring my progress by the labyrinth," she reflected. "At the summer solstice, I could walk the labyrinth half way holding onto Helmut every step. We had the equinox celebration last Saturday and I could walk in and out by myself."

"You two stay and walk," Patty said. "I tell people, 'Just walk as far as you feel like walking, and remember— it's okay to cross the lines.' "

Patty and I stayed in touch only briefly after our visit. When verifying information for her story, I learned of her death. Words on the Redsun Labyrinth website speak eloquently of her legacy:

> "In Memory. The Redsun Labyrinth will forever be in honor and celebration of the life that Patty Meyer brought to this landscape with her dream and vision."

And in Patty's words, "Redsun Labyrinth—A Place of Possibility."

Rebecca Foster
Salmon, Idaho
September 25, 2013

The sky was a milky gray as Mary and I drove from our B&B in Salmon to Rebecca's cabin thirty minutes south. Rock cliffs bordered one side of the highway, the Salmon River the other as we snaked from one curve to the next.

As soon as Rebecca spotted our car, she rushed out of the cabin with a baby carrier strapped to her chest. Wisps of strawberry blond hair peeked out the top.

"I love it that you came! It's such an out-of-the-way place that we don't have many people come walk the labyrinth, or come at all for that matter." She laughed as she led us inside the cabin.

"This is Lilly-O, and this is Joe." We gently patted Lilly-O's head and shook hands with Joe.

"And this is my friend Mary," I added.

"Mary, like I wrote Twylla, we're in the process of adopting Lilly-O. Joe and I used to always say, 'If a baby falls out of the sky, we'll catch it.' Lilly-O came that quickly and unexpectedly. It reminds me of walking the labyrinth. You're not sure where you're going, then all of a sudden you find yourself home.

"It's like a song I wrote about ten years ago. I barely remembered the words until I started walking the labyrinth with Lilly-O. It starts like,

"My life is a labyrinth and it's full of surprises
Where turns to the left are rights in disguises."

Rebecca sang a stanza, repeated the refrain, then hummed before speaking again.

"I've been walking the labyrinth with Lilly-O since she was a week old. I know that its rhythm is going to be a part of her body somehow. She's happiest when she's moving. While she's napping, I'll tell you about the labyrinth."

Rebecca laughed. She laughed often and joyfully.

"Idaho has always been more Joe's place. We live part of the time in Rhode Island and that's where my friends and students are. I teach meditation. The first time we came out here for an extended period of time I thought, 'What am I going to do?' Before we left Providence, we went to a New Year's Eve service at an Episcopal church that had a canvas labyrinth. I was walking it, listening to our friend play the viola and it came to me. 'This is what I'm going to do in Idaho. I'm going to build a labyrinth.'

"I researched all about labyrinths," Rebecca went on. I wanted a Chartres because that's the kind I walked at the church. I forget how I decided on the dimensions; but it's sixty-six feet, rather than the traditional forty-two."

"The labyrinth was how Rebecca connected to this place," Joe noted. "I'm a big fan of it too. It puts you right there in the moment. It's about being alive and experiencing all this beauty."

"Joe's always been very supportive. In fact, it was his strong back that hauled most of the rocks that I used in the labyrinth. I'd go up in the mountains and hunt for rocks, fill backpacks with about fifty pounds, then send Joe up to get them.

"I found special river rocks in and around the Salmon River for the center and turns," Rebecca explained. "Rocks, walking and meditation are all things I love. The labyrinth was my way of bringing them to this place.

"It's a meditation, building a labyrinth," she added quietly.

Lilly-O shifted her position slightly as Rebecca eased from her chair and guided us out the door. The sound of rapidly rushing water grew more intense as we approached the labyrinth, with the banks of the Salmon River mere feet below. Rounded mountains that fringed the immediate area looked like pillows compared to jagged gray peaks in the distance.

Rebecca's labyrinth matched the beauty of the natural landscape as twelve concentric circles of native rock outlined the familiar pattern.

"It's always been my way to ask a question when I enter the labyrinth. You let go of answers as you walk in and allow them to come as you walk out. Now with Lilly-O, I stand in each of the labyrinth's petals and look in a different direction. Something always catches my eye—the bench, the electrical wire—something that gives me insight into my question. It's in the moment."

Rebecca and Lilly-O rounded the second turn, then Mary began. I waited, quietly observing a new mother and baby, my friend with two grown children of her own.

I stepped forward, a mother of three and grandmother of four, and whispered, "Happy Birthday, dear Katherine," to our daughter ... due to deliver a son in three weeks.

EN ROUTE

Salmon, Idaho
Bed and Breakfast
September 25, 2013

SNOW.

Just a coating here, the forecast predicts. But "significantly more" in higher elevations, specifically Lost Trail Pass, exactly where Mary and I are headed in the morning. I'm sure there's a story behind that name like someone got LOST, fell over the edge, his body never discovered.

We successfully cleared the pass yesterday without incident (or drama), but the road was perfectly clear. Nevertheless, I hugged the innermost lane, away from the edge and never looked down.

Earlier this evening I asked Dave, the lodge owner, "Do I need chains? Do you think my car will make it?"

"You'll make it fine," he assured me. "Five miles up; five miles down. Just take your time."

His wife, Paula, patted my arm. "I'm from Mississippi. We never see snow there. If I can do it, anyone can do it."

I imagined the car sliding, swerving, gaining speed, tumbling down thousands of feet—LOST!

Not helpful.

* * *

Mary's House
Sagle, Idaho
September 26, 2013

Light snow flurries grew fatter and faster as Mary and I climbed toward the pass this morning. The windshield wipers flung snow left and right. The road grew steadily whiter.

A heavy truck pulled ahead of us. I settled in behind him, my eyes glued to his black tire prints. I asked Mary to talk, about anything. She is one of the kindest, calmest people I know. Her voice never quivered, never hinted that my panicky behavior made her the least bit nervous.

But to my surprise, my behavior wasn't as panicky as I had expected. The curtain of white served to hide the road's precipitous edge, and our inside lane of traffic felt protected by the bulky base of the mountain. More significant than these strategic advantages, however, was my own mantra. It actually seemed to be working.

"This moment, just this moment."

"This moment, just this moment."

Halfway up, we glimpsed the elevation sign to our right and silently nodded what we both knew. We were on our way down, at twenty miles an hour.

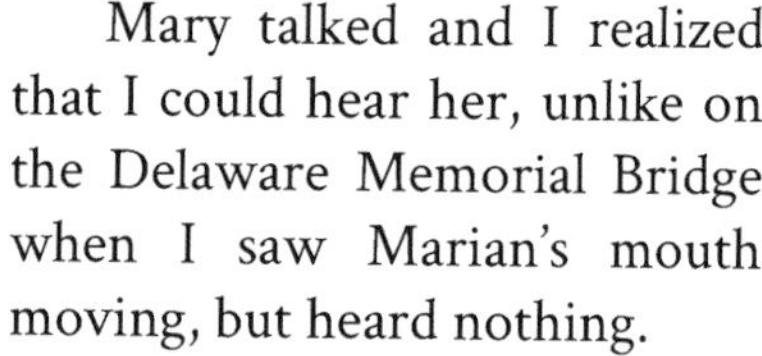

Mary talked and I realized that I could hear her, unlike on the Delaware Memorial Bridge when I saw Marian's mouth moving, but heard nothing.

Fear was still present, hovering near my headrest. But moment by moment I inched it further away, until it perched dangerously close to the glove compartment. With one fell swoop, I shoved it in and slammed the door.

Above the clamor of Fear's irate yet muffled threats, I heard another voice. Clear. Resilient. Excited. My own!

"Only two more miles, Mary. The road's clearing. We're almost there!"

A car behind us honked and passed. The outskirts of Darby, Montana edged into view.

I pulled over in front of a coffee shop, parked, and released my grip on the steering wheel. Coffee! I don't even drink it, but it felt like a celebration.

FIVE UNEVENTFUL HOURS later, we turned into Mary and Doug's driveway.

Before I settled under Mary's homemade quilt tonight, I opened my gratitude journal and wrote what I write every night—five things for which I'm grateful.

A safe drive.

Mary's friendship and calm, caring spirit.

Progress in coping with my fear of heights.

A delicious homemade dinner.

Tomorrow's drive to the Spokane airport is … FLAT, all the way!

13

Close to Home

Kansas, Missouri, Arkansas

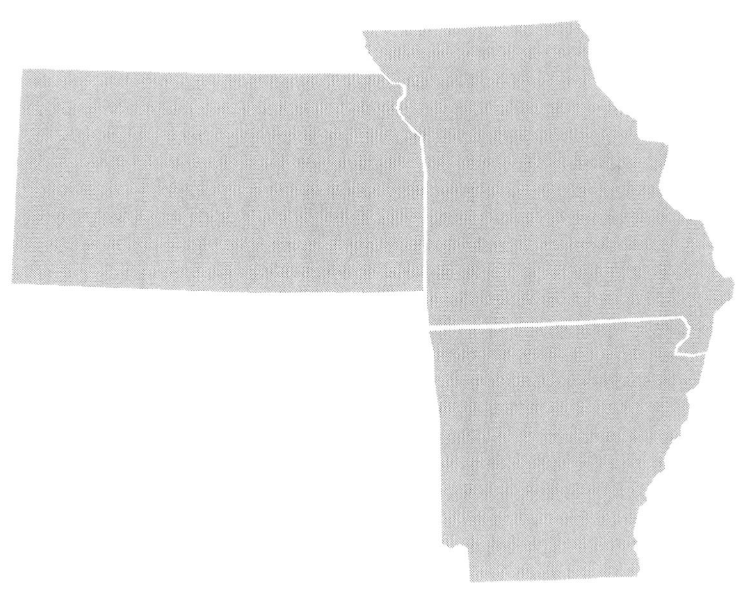

Top, left to right: Joy Freeman, Kansas; Vickie Hall, Arkansas. Right: Ellie Smith, Missouri.

~ Twylla's journal ~

Greenbrier, Arkansas home
November 11, 2013

My own labyrinth could count as the one for Arkansas. It would meet the criteria:

✓ Built and/or envisioned by a woman (me)
✓ Outdoors (our yard)
✓ Non-commercial (nothing business-like about it)

But there's only one problem. It isn't built yet. It's still a vision only I can see.

I know which labyrinth I want—Chartres.

I know how much space I need—forty-two feet.

I've criss-crossed the three acres of available space around our house many times. I've sat on stumps, gazed up at trees, waited for a sign. So far, nothing. No circle of trees or patch of land has said, "This is it. Go get your measuring tape and begin."

Maybe I have too many choices. I laugh when I remember what Janis Buyarski in Juneau said about deciding on a place for her labyrinth: "Blessed are they who have enough land to have options of where to put their labyrinth. Me? Only one flat space."

No, it's not that simple. It's not about having the space or a plan. It's about me. I'm not ready.

Building a labyrinth is a physical as well as emotional and spiritual investment. It deserves time and attention. I have fifteen more women to visit, fifteen more labyrinths to walk before this journey is finished. Then I'll be ready to commit to my own labyrinth, and the land.

Three days from now, I'll check Arkansas off the list when I walk Vickie's labyrinth in Garfield. Before that, I meet Joy then Ellie.

* * *

A trio of friends—Harry Potter, Hermione, Ron—is waiting in the car. On the six-hour drive to Shawnee, Kansas, they'll tell the tale of their adventure in *The Chamber of Secrets.* Let the journey begin!

Joy Freeman
Shawnee, Kansas
November 12, 2013

A late autumn sun was an hour away from setting when I reached Joy's house at 4:00. It hung above the wooden fence in the backyard, shedding light on our conversation for as long as it could. Directly under its dazzling glow lay the labyrinth, a small three-circuit Trinity labyrinth. Joy would soon share its other name.

"I tend to be a person who jumps on the band wagon quickly," Joy began as we sat down at her kitchen table. "But when it came to the labyrinth, I wanted to make sure that it was the real deal, not just some passing spiritual fad in my life. So after my first two walks, I let it sit for a while. I finished seminary and started my chaplaincy residency, but the labyrinth just wouldn't let me go. I kept reading about it, and I even used finger labyrinths with hospital patients in my ministry project. It was clear that the labyrinth was not only going to be a part of my ministry, but my life.

"It was at labyrinth facilitator training with Lauren Artress," Joy continued, "that I knew I wanted a labyrinth of my own. Then we bought this house with such a big backyard, and I said, 'My labyrinth is going right there.' But I didn't have any way of knowing that it would be nine years before we'd actually build it."

We stood to get a clearer view of the labyrinth as the sun balanced gracefully on the upper edge of the fence. One of its rays settled on a white cross positioned to the right of the labyrinth among a row of lavender bushes.

"It's a Celtic cross. My dad's side of the family came from Ireland

and Celtic spirituality has always spoken deeply to my heart. I envisioned it there when I planned the labyrinth, with a path of white rocks outlined with red brick. But all those plans were put on the back burner when Collin's parents and my grandmother became ill and we had our first baby."

Joy proceeded, more slowly, as if deliberately choosing the right words.

"Then fourteen weeks into my second pregnancy, we discovered that our child had severe, unsurvivable congenital anomalies. I had my own health issues, which further increased the risks. So we named the child Hope, without finding out if the baby was a boy or girl. We then made the very difficult decision of letting go of our baby and giving Hope back to God, the only physician who could heal Hope."

Joy placed a hand over her mouth and closed her eyes.

"A year later," she began again, "I was standing at the kitchen window, looking out at the backyard and said to my husband, Collin, 'I can't keep doing this [going through the grief process] without my labyrinth.' I was stuck. Our family was stuck. So we started building the labyrinth, together.

"We all made multiple trips to the hardware store to buy supplies. Collin cleared and prepped the space then we laid the bricks and spread the rocks. The three-circuit design came from John Ritter at Paxworks. The Trinity [Christ, God and the Holy Spirit] is very important to my personal belief system, and the 14-x-14-foot size fit perfectly in the corner by the fence."

Joy opened her labyrinth album and pointed to a photo of a concrete disc with a Celtic cross in the center, decorated with green stones. *Hope's Labyrinth* was scripted across the bottom in Joy's handwriting.

"Hope was the catalyst for building our labyrinth. Part of what I realized during my grieving was that we only had a small memory box with a few cards people had sent, a couple of sonograms—tiny mementos to show that Hope had ever existed. I wasn't okay with that. The labyrinth is a monument to Hope's existence and so much more. It helped us move through our grief."

Joy stood and put on her jacket. "And for me, personally, it's become a centering place. I try to walk it before I go to work. Some days as a chaplain you give everything you have, and then some, helping keep families put together. For me, the labyrinth is my time."

The sun peeked through the fence slats as it inched toward the end of its day. I waited at the labyrinth's entrance while Joy and her daughter walked to the center and hugged. Hope's name stone lay at my feet.

Then a sweet voice that could only come from a sensitive six-year-old, said, "You can feel Hope's heart when you walk the labyrinth."

So I did.

Ellie Smith
Lebanon, Missouri
November 13, 2013

I GRABBED MY purse and the rock beside me on the car seat and walked up the sidewalk to Ellie's front door. The smooth, gray rock had called to me in September when I hiked at the base of Juneau's Mendenhall Glacier. I had no particular plans for it, other than as a fond reminder of our Alaska home, until I read Ellie's website. She, too, had lived in Juneau.

"A Coastal Helicopters t-shirt!" I exclaimed as Ellie opened the door.

"Of course, I had to dress up for your visit," she laughed. "You're the only visitor I've ever had who would know that this came from Alaska, instead of some place like Florida."

Ellie's two cats and dog, Ruby, eavesdropped on our Alaska reminiscences as they lazed around the wood stove. Ruby's ear twitched and eyes fluttered briefly as the talk moved to labyrinths and she heard her name mentioned.

"Ruby's a big fan of the labyrinth. She especially likes to walk it with someone. And thanks to my husband, Jim, you'll actually be able to walk it. It was like a jungle before he cleared it out for your visit."

"If it weren't for Jim and a bad case of the flu, the labyrinth might not have ever been built, or at least when it was," Ellie smiled. "It was 2001 and I was pretty sick, flat on my back, not a very good patient. Jim had to make a trip to Springfield and I told him about a labyrinth book I'd seen in a bookstore there. He came home with two labyrinth books; neither was the one I asked for. But one was all about how to build labyrinths.

"Wait," Ellie said, raising her right hand like she was stopping traffic. "Let me back up a few years.

"I've wanted a labyrinth ever since I walked my first one back in 1989. It was with a group of women in the Berkeley Hills in California during a full moon. We each carried a candle and did a meditation in the center. I was so amazed by the whole experience of walking this pattern in ritual and meditation. I felt changed. I really did. And I went home thinking, 'I want one of these.' It only took me twelve years."

"Now back to The Build."

I tried to keep up.

"So when I was convalescing from the flu, Jim came into the bedroom and casually asked me three questions, which I promptly answered.

"'If you were going to have a labyrinth, where do you think you'd put it?' he asked. 'South of the savanna (a grove of trees we planted),' I said.

"'If you were going to have a labyrinth, how big do you think it should be?' he asked. 'Big! A Chartres design with a path about three feet wide,' I said.

"And finally, 'What would you make it out of?' he asked. 'Rocks.

There's plenty in Missouri,' I said.

"Then when I was still weak but feeling better, he just as casually remarked ...

'You probably need some fresh air.' "

So he ushered me outside and showed me the wheelbarrow full of foot-long sticks he had cut and sharpened.

'What the hell?' I said.

'For staking out your labyrinth,' he answered.

"He had already measured the space and found that it was just the right size for an eleven-circuit labyrinth with a three-foot path!"

ELLIE LAUGHED A deep, long laugh—loud enough to wake up the cats. Ruby's head didn't move from the warm, cushy rug. She'd obviously heard this story before.

"I have to tell you this ... once the string was laid out and the design came into shape—VROOM! The labyrinth's energy came alive.

"Want to meet it?" she asked.

Ruby was up and out the door before I could put on my jacket.

"I LAID EVERY single rock," Ellie pointed out. "Eighteen truck loads!"

Ankle-high grasses grew over and between thousands of Missouri rocks, transforming them into spiky cushions. At the center, Ellie parted one cushion after another to reveal her inner circle of "very special" rocks, one from every state and thirty countries.

"And I'll find just the right spot for yours," she added. "First, I've got to do some clearing. The maintenance can be a pain in the butt sometimes, but I love having it. It has its own energy."

I WONDERED. WAS it the labyrinth's energy that brought me, and my rock, to Ellie? To one of the few people in the world who has ever lived in Juneau, Alaska? Who loves rocks and labyrinths?

Ruby nudged my leg. I took that as a sign.

* * *

EN ROUTE

Bentonville, Arkansas
Hotel
November 13, 2013

"Do you have a ladder I could use to climb up on the roof of this building?" I heard myself ask Ellie this afternoon.

"Sure! Got one right over here," she said as if people climb on her roof all the time.

Granted, the building wasn't that high—maybe eight or nine feet. Still, it was up there. And how else was I supposed to take a picture of the entire labyrinth? It had to be done.

But me? The one who's afraid of heights? I don't do these kinds of things.

Yet, I didn't think twice. I didn't talk myself out of it. I didn't say, "So, Ellie, would you mind climbing up there to take a picture?"

I didn't put myself in that familiar box.

Wow. wow!

Vickie Hall
Garfield, Arkansas
November 14, 2013

"There it is, Vickie's nine-foot bunny!" I announced to myself. I had been on the lookout for it for the last half mile.

The yard has a nine-foot bunny and a place to park, Vickie's directions had specified on the World Wide Labyrinth Locator.

I didn't expect its curly eyelashes and blue sweater.

"Hi! I see you've met Jack," Vickie said as she pointed upwards to a monogram I could barely discern on the rabbit's sweater. It took me a minute to make the connection, then we both laughed. Jack ... Rabbit.

"People like to stop and see him. It's fun! And sometimes I'll point out the labyrinth to them since it's just over there." I followed her gaze to a sea of thick, brown leaves. There wasn't a circle in sight.

"My husband, Mike, is charging the leaf blower and hopefully it'll be ready before you leave. Let's go inside and visit to give it more time to charge."

Had I known a leaf-blower mantra, I would have started repeating it.

"I built the labyrinth, first, on the other side of the house. But the grass kept growing back over the lines and it was really hard to maintain. So I hauled all the rocks over to the east side where the property's in the shade. Ever since then, the labyrinth's been wonderful, except for this time of year when it's covered with leaves, then in the winter when it gets covered with snow."

Vickie smiled and offered me a cup of coffee.

"Mike and I fell in love with this place, mainly because it's so green. We moved here from California where it's dead dry at the end of summer, but here everything's still alive. One of the first people I met had a labyrinth, about a half hour away in Eureka Springs. I'd already walked one in Oregon and had been fascinated by them.

When I saw hers, I said, 'I've got to make one.' So I got a book about labyrinths and picked out the chalice style."

"A chalice? You mean like a cup?"

"Yeah, the center part looks like a cup with a stem and has two openings. The path goes back and forth, as usual, and that's the part I like the best. When you think you're at the end, you're actually at the far edge and you have to come back. It's the symbolism, like life. You go through phases of your life when you think, 'I've almost got it together,' then you find that you don't have it together at all and have to start over. Then you go in a completely different direction. But it all ends up at the same place.

"Then you reverse the whole track," she continued, circling her right index finger in one direction then the other. "It's like reviewing what you've been through. It's a joyful thing!

"The chalice design is easier to explain if you can see it. Let's ask Mike if the blower is charged."

"Hey!" Mike called as he jumped down from the tractor. "The big blower's not ready, but I've got a smaller one that might be powerful enough. The leaves are pretty deep, but I'll give it a try."

Leaves quivered momentarily then leapt out of the way as Mike swept the nozzle from side to side. Like a fast-forwarded film, an entire labyrinth magically appeared before our eyes in less than fifteen minutes.

"All these things you see along the path have just hit me at one point or another and I've said, 'This belongs in the labyrinth.' Vickie straightened a bird cage, dusted off a glass ball atop a pedestal and gently stroked the heads of three statues, all women. "My labyrinth's pretty much dedicated to the female aspect of things."

I joined her on the concrete bench in the center. "I haven't walked the labyrinth in five or six months," she shared. "I have a ruptured disc in my low back and when it flares up, I'm done. I try to get out here so I can calm down and get focused, but it's been hard for me to do. When I'm in the labyrinth, though, Mike knows—no phone, nothing—is supposed to bother me.

"I like to watch other people walk it. Some like to dance and skip through it and laugh. It's a real comfortable place to be, a sacred place, so to speak."

I looked up at the overhanging oak limbs. Some were empty, but others still clung fiercely to their leaves. In another week the ground would be covered again, its treasures hidden. The labyrinth would be at rest. Only Vickie, Mike—and Jack—would know of its presence.

14

To Go or Not to Go?

Kentucky, Tennessee, Mississippi

Top, left to right: Clarice O'Bryan, Kentucky ; Nancy Bridges, Mississippi. Right: Gracie Regen, Tennessee.

~Twylla's journal~

Liberty International Airport, New Jersey
February 17, 2014

THE DEPARTURE BOARD says *On Time* beside our flight to Nashville, but I'm holding my breath until we actually take off. The Polar Vortex is pounding parts of the country with record snowfall, rainfall, and extreme cold. People stranded at airports for days is disconcerting. But we're headed south to Kentucky, Tennessee and even deeper south to Mississippi.

"We'll be fine," I assured Marian, and she believed me … until we saw the forecast last night. A nor'easter is headed toward the east coast, predicting major snow and ice storms as far south as Louisiana.

Then came the email from Clarice in Kentucky, whose labyrinth we're (supposedly) visiting tomorrow:

> "I awoke this morning to over three inches of snow. The labyrinth has disappeared. Hope we have a clear view on the eighteenth."

Followed by the email from Gracie in Tennessee:

> "The labyrinth is covered with soggy, heavy leaves. More rain is forecast, maybe severe."

Nothing yet from Nancy in Mississippi. A good sign.

Should we cancel? Take our chances?

"Go for it!" the Thelma and Louise voices cheer.

"This is a pre-boarding announcement for Southwest flight #723 with non-stop service to Nashville."

And we're off!

* * *

EN ROUTE

Knob Creek Farm, Kentucky
Abraham Lincoln's boyhood home
February 17, 2014

MARIAN GRACIOUSLY INDULGED my Lincoln fascination. We'd already detoured sixty miles off our route to see Lincoln's birthplace. But that site wasn't what I hoped it would be. It was too grand and staged, with a replica of Lincoln's birth cabin enshrined in a granite memorial framed with dramatic columns.

"There *is* his boyhood home," the park ranger offered, "about ten miles down the road," but it'd be real muddy out there after all the snow. Not much to see, just a couple of cabins and land."

Exactly. Land!

I'd read Carl Sandburg's *Abraham Lincoln: The Prairie Years and The War Years,* Gore Vidal's *Lincoln, a Novel,* Doris Kearns Goodwin's *A Team of Rivals* and more. But there remained one unanswered question that no author could answer for me. I needed to *feel* the answer for myself as I stood on the same land where Lincoln stood.

Wearing knee-high rain boots, I mucked through mud from the car to a replica of another Lincoln log cabin. A one-room square, with one window and one door, this crude cabin was where the young Abraham lived with his family from ages two and a half to almost eight.

"My earliest recollection is of the Knob Creek place," a marker quoted Lincoln.

I followed a split rail fence toward the swollen Knob Creek, as far as the mud would allow, then turned to look back over a wide cleared field behind Lincoln's cabin. I pictured a young boy, about the age of two of our grandsons, chasing his sister Sarah. They stopped to help their mother, Nancy, pull weeds in the garden. Abe carried a load of logs from the woodpile to the house, stacked it beside the door then returned to get another, then another.

My question begged an answer. On this land where Lincoln worked long days, played, walked miles to school, mourned the death of an infant brother and grew in body and mind …

What did he take away with him that shaped who he was and who he would become?

He surely learned determination, perseverance and resilience.

But was there something more, a virtue that would transcend them all, that would allow Lincoln to look beyond the present to what could be—in his own life and in the life of a country?

My imagination returned to young Abe. He leaned comfortably against the trunk of an oak tree, its branches shading him from the noon day sun. He opened a thick book bound in black, the family Bible, that his mother read aloud to him and Sarah each night. His eyes lingered on the words, lightly tracing them with his fingertips, then his gaze shifted to the land. Once more his attention alternated, slowly, between land and book. Then he gently closed the cover, rubbed his right hand over it and smiled, ever so slightly.

And in that brief moment, I glimpsed the *more.*

Lincoln learned…

to dream.

◊◊◊

Clarice O'Bryan
Owensboro, Kentucky
February 18, 2014

"Clarice, this is Twylla. Marian and I are at the Hampton Inn in Owensboro. We can be at your house in about twenty minutes."

"Great! The rain last night cleared a lot of snow off the labyrinth and the sun is shining for the first time in about ten days!" she exclaimed. Her excitement mirrored my own.

"I've brewed us some labyrinth tea," Clarice said as the three of us sat at her kitchen table. "See the labyrinth on the front of the tin?

"When you parked in the driveway, you probably noticed that there are still several patches of snow on the labyrinth. But I think you'll be able to walk it, real carefully.

"And did you see the seven trees circling it? That's why I named it the Sacred Oak Grove Labyrinth. That's been ... let's see ... about seventeen or eighteen years ago now," Clarice said slowly, as if adding up the years in her head. Over 3,000 pilgrims have walked it."

Clarice took half a sip of tea then laughed. "I have a funny story concerning how I decided to create it. At the labyrinth dedication, my husband spoke and asked the crowd, 'Do you know what frightens a husband more than anything in the world? It's when his wife sits up in bed and says, 'Honey, I had a vision.' "

"A vision?" Marian asked.

"Yes, I saw it, just as plain as day, a Chartres labyrinth right where it is now. I believe the vision came as the answer to my mission statement—to create something where people could come together, diverse people, and have a common experience, a common spiritual experience. We're in the buckle of the Bible Belt here, you know.

"Building it, well, that took about eight months," Clarice added, with a slight smile and shake of the head.

"I hired a man who thought it was going to be a piece of cake, but then he realized that it was just too much work. That evening I asked the Divine Mother, to whom the labyrinth is dedicated, to help me. The very next morning I met Joyce Fitzgerald, a restoration biologist, who agreed to take the job. She dug the holes and placed the stones while I wheelbarrowed the dirt out. I was sixty-two at the time and shouldn't have been lifting those heavy loads, but I did!

"You know what we buried in the center?" she asked. "An eight-foot long snake which had been run over by a car. We buried it with great ceremony, adorning it with herbs and crystals and built an altar over it. The serpent is the symbol of ancient feminine wisdom."

I tried to remain calm. Whoever crowned snakes the symbol of feminine wisdom obviously didn't shake at the sight of one.

"We thought it was going to take sixteen tons of sandstone for the path," Clarice continued, "but we found that we needed twice that amount. I put all the costs on my credit card and eventually paid it off. When there is an inner knowing that I need to do something, I go with it, no matter what.

"Probably what you're feeling right now," Clarice said, speaking directly to me.

I hadn't expected the conversation to turn in my direction, but Clarice was right. The further I traveled my path, the stronger I trusted my own inner knowing.

"I used to do psychic readings," she explained. "I don't do them anymore, or I don't call them that because I prefer to lead a person to their own answers. Instead, I call the process guided imagery. Tonight I have a group of twelve women coming here for a workshop on Receiving Love. I'll lead a guided meditation, we'll share, drum and maybe dance ancient dances.

"We can't dance on the labyrinth today," she laughed, "but I'll get my wrap and boots and we'll go take a look."

A thin glaze of ice clung to most of the sandstone path, but the stained-glass healing stone (caduceus) that Clarice had created for the entrance was clear. She proudly pointed to a sculpture which stood slightly off-center. "My son, Shane Smith, created it for the labyrinth. It's titled The Greening of the Mind, Body, and Spirit."

"If I don't have a particular intention when I walk, I'll ask to open my heart more," she offered. "We're always talking about giving—giving energy, giving light, giving healing. I'm coming to see how important it is to receive it all. Receiving love, after all, is loving yourself."

With no particular intention of my own, I embraced Clarice's suggestion to open my heart, to receive the energy of her labyrinth and absorb the wisdom of her words. And to take her practical advice, to walk "real carefully."

Gracie Regen
Nashville, Tennessee
February 18, 2014

We had missed the address twice when Marian shouted, "There it is! Back up."

Overcast clouds blanketed a hillside of trees to conceal all but the tiniest speck of Gracie's white house. The car clattered across wooden slats separating us from a creek bed as we maneuvered the narrow driveway.

"I'm glad you could make it," Gracie said as we parked at the top of the hill, "but I won't be able to stay out here with you very long. My back's giving me problems and I'll need to go back inside and rest soon. I brought you information about The Man in the Maze labyrinth that'll answer some of your questions."

Gracie handed me a sheet of paper on her way toward a flat clearing sandwiched between two steep hills. The faint outline of her labyrinth was visible beneath a patchy layer of brown leaves.

"A substantial wind blew through yesterday, otherwise you wouldn't be able to make it out," Gracie explained, kicking leaves off her boots. "I've been taking care of this land for eight years—pulling out vines, invasives, privets and positioning trees to prevent flooding. For me it's total one hundred percent stewardship, especially of the trees. I believe I was sent here. I tend the labyrinth more than walk it.

"I intended to put a Chartres labyrinth back here," she went on, "but the spirits said, 'No, we don't want a Chartres. We want you to build a Native American labyrinth.' I didn't even know there was such a thing. I called my friend Sarah, who does, and she explained the Man in the Maze to me. Of course it's not really a maze. But Native Americans called it that because life is confusing and it can feel like a maze to get through.

"You see the driveway there?" Gracie asked. "I've learned that everything on this side of it belongs to the spirits, not to me. I pay the rent, but it's theirs. There's really strong energy here."

She turned in the opposite direction and faced nine large, gray stones at the far edge of the labyrinth.

"I got those stones for people to sit on. They came from the foundation of slave cabins, hand-carved by slaves. Some of their spirits are standing there now. I'm a seer," she explained. "I see forms, outlines, like if you're driving on a long, hot road and you see vapors come up. I don't make out details like clothes or jewelry the people are wearing.

"I need to get off my feet for a few minutes," Gracie announced suddenly, walking stiffly toward the house. "I'll leave you here to explore. Grayfeather will be with you. He's a sentinel."

Marian followed her to get a drink of water and I was left alone. Or perhaps not. I could not see what Gracie saw, but the thought of a friendly presence hanging out with me was oddly comforting. I climbed one hill then the other, pausing to take pictures of the labyrinth from a higher perspective.

Leaves crunched under my feet as I stepped into the first, and only, Man in the Maze I would walk on my fifty-state journey. In the center I unfolded Gracie's paper.

"... [The Man in the Maze] is equivalent to the classical seven

> circuit labyrinth. It is commonly seen in the Tohono O'odham Nation (Native American tribe) of the Central Valley in Arizona. The little man [in the center] is named "U'ki'ut'l" in their language. There is no one meaning. A common interpretation is that the figure stands for the O'odham people (or more broadly an individual or mankind). The 'maze' represents the difficult journey toward finding deeper meaning in life."

The back door slammed and Gracie emerged carrying a wooden box. "It's my supplies for the prayer tree over there," she said. "I invite people who walk the labyrinth to write a prayer, tie it with one of these ribbons and place it on the tree.

"And did I tell you that I blessed all the rocks around the labyrinth? Spirit said, 'You need to charge water and bless each rock with wisdom, love and peace.' So I wrote those words on bottles of water and placed them in the sun. Then I blessed each rock with the charged water. It took lots of water!"

Abruptly changing the subject, Gracie said, "I'll be moving to Indiana soon. If people who buy the place don't have any interest in the labyrinth, I guess I'll have to close it down. Or will I? Its energy will always be here."

The labyrinth's energy would remain, but it would never be alone. Marian and I tied our prayers on the tree and waved good-bye ... to all.

Nancy Bridges
Tupelo, Mississippi
February 19, 2014

Marian rang the doorbell for the second time as I walked toward an expansive, flat piece of land to the left of the house.

"It's a labyrinth!" I shouted. "We're in the right place." Brown grass, cropped as close as a buzz cut, covered the area, interrupted only by brick pavers outlining the path. My phone rang. It was Nancy.

"Sorry I'm running late. I'll be there in five minutes." Not only had she switched an appointment to accommodate our schedule, but had left work to meet us. We welcomed Nancy to her own front porch then followed her inside to visit.

"I discovered your labyrinth while we were waiting." I said. The Labyrinth Locator lists it as one hundred feet across and it looks every bit of that."

"Yes, it is. I wanted a two-foot path with two feet in between so I could put pavers and flowers, so it just kept growing and growing. I mostly plant tulips between the pavers and a few wildflowers. Spring and summer are my favorite times to walk it. My husband helped me lay it out. We marked the circles and turns then dug a trench for the pavers. We finished it in just a little more than a weekend."

Nancy's phone rang. She glanced at the caller—her office —but remained focused on her guests.

"I knew I wanted an eleven-circuit because that's the first one I walked on a retreat in St. Louis, plus we had the space for one. But what I really wanted is not what I got," Nancy laughed.

"I wanted it to be further away from the house and on a slope, lower at the entrance then slanting up in the walk, so you would gradually see the pond in the distance. But my husband thought it would be better on flat ground, and in doing that, it's closer to the house."

Nancy walked across the living room to a window overlooking the labyrinth and pointed to the flatscreen TV overhead. "When I used to first walk the labyrinth in the evenings, I'd see and hear this big blankety-blank TV. One night I was out there walking, getting really agitated, wishing my labyrinth was further away from the house, when the perfect name for it came to me. *Harmony*—to be okay with what is. The labyrinth has become like a melding of my life and work, of the spiritual and physical."

She sighed, not so much from relief as contentment and returned to her chair. "The labyrinth's been a good teaching tool in that way. I've learned to let things be a little more.

"And now after nine years," she said with a sly smile, "the bushes have grown up so tall that you don't notice the TV any more. I was walking the labyrinth last night before you came and couldn't tell the TV was on. So life is even better!

"There is one sound that brings me a lot of pleasure while I walk—my wind chimes. There's enough of a breeze now that you'll be able to hear them."

The labyrinth appeared dormant, awaiting new life. It would be at least another month in Mississippi before tiny green shoots would emerge between the pavers. Two black wrought iron chairs and a table marked the center. Nancy's wind chimes tinkled softly. All else was quiet.

Nancy stepped a few feet into the labyrinth, turned and said, "I had a real special experience here when the youth group from our church walked the labyrinth. I performed a ceremony and gave them all journals to write about their thoughts and feelings.

"There were two senior boys in the group," she continued. "One walked out crying and said, 'I don't know what it was that made me cry.' The other asked if I would sponsor his senior project and help him build a labyrinth at the church. I did. We laid it out, put down tarp, mulch and rocks along the path. It was well received, although there are probably some people who think it's voodoo, but ... oh, well.

"It's just such a sense of peace, walking it," she reflected, "and I'm so grateful I could pass it on.

"But right now, I'm sorry to say that I have to rush back to work. I hope you'll stay and enjoy a peaceful walk."

Marian meandered to the center and sat in one of the chairs. I stepped through the entrance. Nancy honked as she passed on the road and we waved back. Somewhere along the outer ring, I caught an unexpected whiff of wild onion, a smell I remembered from early spring days in Arkansas. The earth was waking up.

~ Twylla's journal ~

Nashville International Airport
February 19, 2013

BACK IN NASHVILLE. We checked in at the Southwest counter. Our flight coming from Chicago had been canceled.

"At least we did it. We visited them all before the weather stopped us." I told Marian, who was already Googling nearby hotels.

"Oh, wait!" shouted the ticket agent. "Flight #45 from Houston is making an unscheduled stop to pick up forty of you going to Newark. I've never known that to happen before."

Somehow, it didn't surprise me a bit!

15

Texas or Bust

Texas

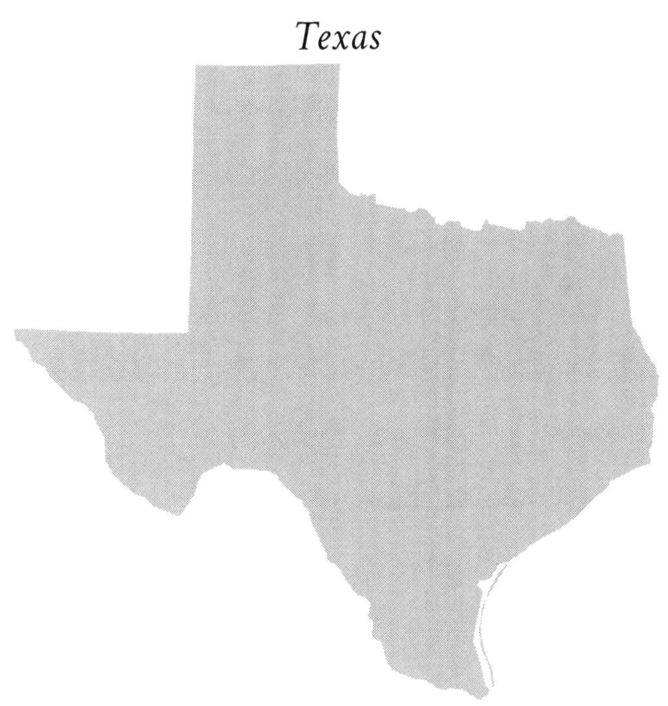

Carolyn Hewitt, Texas.

~ Twylla's journal ~

March 17, 2014
Little Rock National Airport, Arkansas

One-hour drive from our Greenbrier home to the airport
One-hour flight to Dallas
Rent car
Forty-minute drive to McKinney
Arrive at Carolyn's by 10:45
Visit
Reverse
Home by 7:30

I planned to drive—six hours there, six hours back—but a $69-each-way ticket turned the tide.

Harry Potter and friends will have to wait until May to continue telling their story. There will be plenty of time then, though, during my six-state marathon. Today, one state feels just right.

Carolyn Hewitt
McKinney, Texas
March 17, 2014

I eased the car into Carolyn's suburban driveway and proceeded to gather up phone, purse and papers. Before I could unbuckle the seatbelt, three sharp knocks sounded on the driver's side window. I turned to see a smiling face framed by snow white hair ... a soul mate, or rather, a hair mate.

"Hey neighbor!" Carolyn called. "Can I help you with anything?"

"Thanks, but I think I've got it." I replied, closing the car door behind me.

"Texas must feel like next door after all your traveling. Come on in and have some water."

Carolyn pointed to two chairs in her den. I noticed that a platter-sized finger labyrinth was propped up against the chair she chose. The pattern's white background, accented with splotches of pastel colors, gleamed from lights overhead.

"I haven't walked my labyrinth in the backyard much this winter, but I use this finger labyrinth almost every day. It's a really powerful tool for me. It calms me down, kind of like meditation or contemplative prayer.

"But labyrinths came to me artistically first," Carolyn explained. "Art was part of my business—redecorating houses, refurbishing, faux finish, that kind of thing. Our church's parish hall hadn't been remodeled in about twenty-five or thirty years and was looking pretty bad. So I volunteered to paint it, change out the carpet, give it an overall facelift. Then one night I had a dream, or just woke up with the thought, that I had to put a labyrinth on the floor. I hadn't even walked one in about ten years, but it was the design that I pictured.

"Once the labyrinth was finished, I realized I didn't know what I was going to do with it!" Carolyn laughed. "How was I going to explain it? I went online and read about them and found Lauren Artress on the Veriditas webpage. She was offering a workshop in St. Paul, Minnesota in the next few weeks. I told my husband, 'I gotta go to St. Paul,' so I flew there and got my facilitator training then my certification."

"You're a labyrinth facilitator too?" I said, feeling the rush of familiarity that flows from shared experience. "I don't know about you, but Lauren's training really solidified my personal relationship with the labyrinth."

"Absolutely! That was the beginning for me. I came home and decided to build my labyrinth. And I'm positive the labyrinth is what set me on a new path. I started exploring the spiritual side of the labyrinth and spiritual growth in my life. In my research, I found that the Stanton Center for Ministry in Dallas offers certification for Spirituality and Spiritual Director.

"I was scared to death to take the classes," she laughed. "I remember talking to my husband and our priest about it. 'I'm seventy-three years old,' I said 'and haven't taken a heavy class in a long time.' One of them said, 'If you take the classes, in four years (that's how long the certification program was), you'll have gained a lot more knowledge. If you don't, you'll be four years older.'

"When he put it like that, I thought, 'I'll do it,' and I did! Even if it was just *for my benefit* (air quotes), or if I *did something* (more air quotes) with the training, it didn't matter. It wasn't a choice. I *had* to.

"BUT I HAVEN'T told you about my own labyrinth yet. I designed it."

Her phone rang.

"My husband," Carolyn said. "He's at a doctor's appointment and is ready for me to pick him up, but I can finish the rest of this story first. You can walk the labyrinth while I'm gone.

"I designed the labyrinth myself on graph paper. It's a five-circuit because that's all the space I had. I marked the path then walked it. But it didn't feel right, so I changed the design and walked it again. My husband, our son and one of his friends got all the rocks and stones for the path and set them in place.

"Now, I'd better go pick up Tony," she said hurriedly, leading the way out the back door.

"Oh, when I come back, I'll tell you about how I started designing labyrinths for other people and about the retreats my daughter, Christine, and I lead called Creative Spirituality."

The large oak in the middle of Carolyn's labyrinth immediately reminded me of her, its limbs spread wide in a neighborly welcome. I followed stepping stones to the center and settled onto the bench. I rested while I could. Soon, Carolyn would return with her amazing, ageless energy. Never let white hair fool you.

16

The Big Push

Nevada, Utah, Wyoming, Colorado, Arizona, New Mexico

Top, right to left: Sarah Sweetwater, Nevada; Cherylee Brewer, Arizona. Middle row, left to right: Vanda Edington, Wyoming; Liz Paterson, New Mexico; Barbara Machann and Mary Turner, Colorado. Right: Peggy Montrone and Christy Montrone-Burns, Utah.

~ Twylla's journal ~

Manhattan apartment
May 5, 2014

I KNEW THIS trip would eventually come, to those far-flung western states where land seems to (and does) stretch on forever. Where towns, much less labyrinths, can be few and far between. I've been fretting about it for months and actively planning it for three weeks. All the logistics—visits, flights, car rentals, hotels—have been pieces of a paper puzzle littering our living room floor.

Just the geography of the area! I needed to double-check: Is Colorado connected to Nevada or Utah? If I fly into Salt Lake City, is that closer to Wyoming or Arizona?

It's embarrassing. But the six states are now emblazoned on my brain, all arrangements are made, and I leave at 6:15 a.m.

With the trip only hours away, I realize that I actually haven't fretted in … about three weeks.

Fret—to constantly worry or be anxious—a word handed down from my mother.

"It's not worth fretting about," or, "Are you still fretting about that?" she'd say.

"No, Mama," I could tell her tonight. "*Fretting* has been edged out, replaced by another verb. *Doing*."

Doing has little time for fretting. It's too busy doing.

It feels powerful.

Sarah Sweetwater
Elko, Nevada
May 7, 2014

IT WAS PROBABLY just the power of suggestion that triggered my taste buds to scream "SALTY!" all the way from Salt Lake City to Elko. The

Great Salt Lake, the Great Salt Lake Desert, the Bonneville Salt Flats. I was tempted to pull off I-80 and pick up a few samples, but it was raining and Sarah was waiting.

"Finally, we meet! What's it been, a year that we've been trying to do this?" Sarah laughed as she opened the sliding glass front door.

"Almost. I called you last August when I was putting together my trip to Idaho, but you were out of town."

"Come on in and I'll grab my jacket, then we can go visit the labyrinths. I have two, you know. I think we'll go to the Peace Labyrinth first."

We stepped into Sarah's house which looked more like a museum, because it is.

"The Sweetwater Bunkhouse," she calls it. Upstairs and down are filled with pieces by local artists, treasures from Sarah's international travels and her own sculptures.

"This is my work-in-progress," she said, proudly pointing to the sculpture of a woman captured seconds before she sits on a bus seat. Rosa Parks. I was captivated by the details: Rosa's long coat, purse, wire-rimmed glasses, braid barely visible under her hat, and eyes looking up—at the bus driver, perhaps?

"I like to carve women like Rosa and Sarah Winnemucca over here," she gestured toward a bronze sculpture on a table near by. "Sarah was a strong voice for her people, the Paiute, living in a dominant white culture.

"This one is Maya, the white marble goddess. I sculpted her from a piece of Carrera marble. She's a compilation of goddess qualities, women of strength and power.

"My hope is that people's lives are changed, broadened you might say, from looking at one of my sculptures. I could talk about art forever but we need to go see the labyrinths," she laughed.

And I could have remained in the presence of "Sarah's women," forever inspired.

"I've designed other labyrinths," Sarah explained as she parked her truck in front of an expansive brick and paver labyrinth, flanked on three sides by an amphitheater. "But this is the first one with angles. It's a nine-circuit classical labyrinth with four quadrants like a Chartres. I designed it to have as many right turns as left, to re-align the body and focus on the inward path for healing.

"And take a look at the center. Peace is engraved in eighty-two languages, as many as I could find. I'll let you in on a secret. Right here is my signature," she whispered.

Double S's, no larger than a dollar coin, appeared as birds in flight or a road curving between two mountain peaks, creating a joyful sensation of movement and freedom.

"This labyrinth is for the public; mine is much more personal. I'll take you over there after we walk this one," Sarah said.

Half an hour later, passing the corner of Silver and Sweetwater streets, I knew we must be close to Sarah's second labyrinth.

Pointing to a building out the driver's side window, Sarah announced, "My sculpture studio's there and my labyrinth's just down the street. My grandkids, some friends and art students helped me build it in 1999 to walk out the old millennium and walk in the new.

"That's how it started," she continued as we walked toward circles of bright white rocks. "But since then, the labyrinth has become sort of mysterious to me. When I walk it and ask a question, the answer comes bubbling up. It's like my feet are connected to an energy source in the ground. It doesn't always happen but when I feel that energy coming up through my feet, I'm connected to the whole rest of the universe. It changes me."

Sarah crossed directly to the center where a collection of objects peaked her curiosity. She bent over to retrieve a small heart-shaped stone, fragment of turquoise, and dried flower.

"I can always tell when a certain student has been here," she smiled. "She leaves me a flower."

Undoubtedly, it was a sign that one woman's life had once again been inspired by another.

I have experienced this inspiration for myself now … forty-seven times.

A YEAR AND a half after my visit, Sarah died of cancer. I did not know of her illness nor learn of her death until I finished this story and wrote to ask about Rosa. Sarah's creative and generous spirit deeply touched my life and will continue to speak to each person who walks her labyrinths, is inspired by her art, and hears her story.

Peggy Montrone
Salt Lake City, Utah
May 8, 2014

"THE LABYRINTH'S AT our cabin in the mountains," Peggy said when she picked me up at the hotel. "The road's open, but there may still be some snow." Her confident demeanor and four-wheel-drive SUV calmed momentary flashbacks to my snowy encounter on Lost Trail Pass in Idaho.

"Christy and I are so interested to hear about your journey," Peggy said, as we drove toward her daughter's house. "She's the one who designed the labyrinth at our cabin and was our leader the day we built it. I want her to tell you all about that part, plus she has some tea and muffins ready for us."

Mid-morning sunshine streamed through the windows of Christy's dining room as she stacked four albums of labyrinth memories on the table. As she opened the top album to a bookmarked page, I remarked, "A person who actually organizes items in albums. Very impressive!"

"This was the first labyrinth we walked in Philo, California," Christy explained. I had read an article about it in a magazine. I thought it would be a cool Mother's Day present for my mother, sisters and sister-in-law to walk one, so we made the trek to Mendocino, drove up a super winding road and walked this labyrinth. It was really fun and I fell in love with them. They're so beautiful and peaceful, and I love circles. I use them a lot in my jewelry designs."

"Christy wanted to learn how to make labyrinths, so we went to Grace Cathedral in San Francisco for a workshop. Then we attended Labyrinth Facilitator Training with Lauren Artress at Chartres Cathedral in France. After that, we started talking about building one at the cabin," Peggy added.

"I'll bet you've never seen someone create a labyrinth by placing an upside down flower pot in the center, with a dowel sticking out the hole and a string attached to it," Christy laughed. "It worked! I walked in circles and sprayed the lines—with environmentally okay paint—then we laid rope to mark the path, except the center and outer-most line. We rimmed those with area rocks."

Peggy flipped through pages until she found the photos she was looking for—women in shorts and hats bending, circling, spray painting grass, laying rope and wiping their brows. "The cabin was a perfect place to build it," she said. "It's centering just knowing the labyrinth's there."

"Yeah, that's the biggest thing, just knowing it's there," Christy agreed. "Even when I'm loading and unloading the car, it's right there. It's official!"

"And don't forget the animals. They like it, too. Remember that moose that lay down in the middle like he was totally comfortable?" Peggy asked. "Now it feels like a sacred space."

"You'd better get going," Christy said. "Take my boots. The ground will be muddy this time of year."

Half an hour past Park City, Peggy turned into Weber Canyon and started the curving climb to the cabin. The higher we drove into the cloud, the faster and larger the snowflakes swirled. Peggy concentrated on the narrow strip of dirt and gravel road directly ahead.

At least twenty-five switchbacks later (not that I was counting), she stopped in front of a cabin surrounded by forest.

"Made it." she exhaled. "It helps that the road crew spread gravel recently, but I don't feel too comfortable staying more than about five minutes as fast as this snow is coming down."

If she didn't, I didn't.

"Can you see the labyrinth, over there in that clearing?"

"Yes, there's a part near the center that's not covered with snow. I'll just take a few pictures, then we can leave."

Peggy guided the car cautiously down the mountain and back to Park City, where the sun was shining. I noticed throughout our lunch that she frequently glanced toward the mountain. As we finished our final sips of tea, Peggy asked a question I could never have anticipated.

"Would you like to go back?"

"Go back?"

"Yes, the sun has broken through that cloud over the mountain so the drive should be clear this time. I'm happy to do it. I know what it's like to have a goal. You want to walk each labyrinth you visit, and we can make it happen. There's plenty of time before your flight to Denver."

I only hoped I could be as generous to someone else one day.

"Yes, Peggy, I'd love to. Thank you!"

THE SNOW HAD melted into a chocolatey soup of mud upon our return. Sunshine highlighted the heads of budding daffodils. Tiny birds flitted from tree to tree. Peggy cheered as I slipped on Christy's boots and slogged my way around their labyrinth, a mother-daughter labyrinth created on a mountain in Utah.

* * *

EN ROUTE

Denver, Colorado
Hotel
May 8, 2014
Mother's Day Flowers, Part 1

"I HAVE A reservation," I told the hotel clerk. "The last name is Alexander."

"Twylla Alexander? Oh, it's you! I've been expecting you."

So this is what celebrities must feel like.

She went into an adjoining office and returned with a long purple box. 1-800-Flowers.

"For me? Are you sure?"

"Yes, your name's right here. They were delivered this afternoon."

As soon as I reached my room, I opened the envelope.

> *We all love you and are very proud of you as you continue on this labyrinth journey! Happy Mother's Day!*
>
> *– Drew, Jason & Kate, Elizabeth & Ben, Katherine & Andy, Luke, Nate, Ruby, Anna, and Robert*

Who thinks to look up his wife's itinerary, the name of her hotel, and arrange for flowers to be waiting when she arrives? Drew!

Where were the tissues?

It was only then that I looked more carefully around the room. Scuff marks on the wall, stain on the carpet, cracked caulking around the bathtub. How had I missed this on Trip Advisor? Everyone in my family knows, all too well, that I'm a "clean hotel fanatic." And my reservation is for three nights!

I placed the flower box on the air conditioning unit, pulled out my laptop and got to work. Within twenty minutes, I had a new reservation at another hotel (4.5 rating on Trip Advisor) down the road.

I cancelled my reservation here and unpacked just enough belongings to get through the night.

But I needed a flower plan.

I won't unpack the box tonight, I strategized, because I'm taking the shuttle to the airport in the morning, renting a car, driving to Cheyenne and back, then checking into the new hotel. The flowers are in individual vials and will survive until I get to Vanda's house in Cheyenne. I'll open the box there, put the flowers in a vase and bring them back.

I'm sure it will totally work.

Vanda Edington
Cheyenne, Wyoming
May 9, 2014

On the surface, the Cheyenne Botanic Gardens—a public institution—wasn't a likely candidate for my visit. But it is outdoors and only three hours from Denver so it fit into my six-state travel puzzle. What about the woman creator? The Labyrinth Locator listed "Rachel Preston Frazier & Labyrinth Committee" as builder; however, Rachel is not who I'm visiting today.

"You didn't have to bring me flowers," Vanda joked as she answered my knock.

I had called ahead to clarify directions and mentioned my flower plan. Vanda had clippers ready. As we talked travel and grandchildren, I snipped the stems of eighteen elegant roses and transferred them from vials to vase.

"Flowers are some of my favorite subjects to paint with pastels, and these soft rose colors would make a lovely picture," Vanda observed.

"That's how I located you, through your artist's website. When I couldn't find contact information for Rachel, I happened upon your name in an article about the labyrinth."

"I'm delighted you found me, but I'm only one of the women involved in creating the labyrinths at the Botanic Gardens. Rachel designed the second one."

"The second one?"

Vanda opened a scrapbook of newspaper clippings. "Here are pictures of the permanent paver labyrinth that you'll see today, but there was originally a grass labyrinth underneath."

"Maybe I'd better back up," she said.

I nodded and reached for a chocolate chip cookie from a plate on the counter.

"I had walked a couple of labyrinths, the first at a Methodist church here. I have to tell you a funny story about that. The lady who was facilitating the walk said to me, 'That's the fastest I've ever seen anyone walk this labyrinth.' It was like I just had to get it done. It was so profound like the labyrinth design was in my psyche, all its swirls and the turning back."

Vanda refreshed our tea cups. "Now back to the Botanic Gardens story.

"I was on the Board and suggested we build a labyrinth. No one got too excited. But one of the members told me about Anne Wagner and Do Palma, who were also interested in labyrinths. I searched them out and we started to talk. Long story short, we came back to the Board with a proposal to partner with the Gardens and build a grass labyrinth for the community. They agreed. That was in 2001.

"It was really a grass roots project," she smiled slyly. "We got directions from the internet, marked if off with kitchen flour, then ground out the path. Everyone seemed to love it."

"Then ..."

I helped myself to a second cookie.

"In 2006 the Board decided to build a more permanent labyrinth, so they created a new committee and I was on it. We selected Rachel, who specializes in spiritual architecture, to design it. I'll give *some* credit to the men who did the digging and laid the stones.

"So, let's go see it! Anne Wagner's going to meet us there. Unfortunately, Do is in Denver today, and Rachel has moved to New Mexico."

I positioned the vase in the front seat floorboard (snug in its custom box fashioned by Vanda's husband, Don) and followed Vanda to the Botanic Gardens. Anne met us at the labyrinth entrance between two century-old apple trees.

"Hi Twylla. Thank you for being the motivation behind all the lovely memories I've been having about building the labyrinth," Anne said. "Vanda and I don't see each other that much; but when we do, this labyrinth is our memory."

"Anne and I came back together a couple of years ago to plan the walk for World Labyrinth Day," Vanda explained. "We felt so gratified to see people in the community using it."

"And it all started from our own personal experiences. When Do and I first became interested in labyrinths," Anne recalled, "it was the centering process, the grounding that made sense to us. It was a time in both our lives when we were trying to figure some things out and the labyrinth was a tool."

She glanced around at the trees, the rounded gate and memorial benches. "I enjoy taking my time on the path, looking up as I walk at the different vistas. They change all along the way, like life."

Vanda patted Anne on the arm, "And you know me, such a Type A. I usually take off at my usual fast pace, but the labyrinth reminds me to slow down and appreciate the journey."

Two labyrinths, one making way for the other, shared roots grounded in women's personal stories. Now a common path for a diverse community, the labyrinth welcomes all walkers—slow, fast or anywhere in between.

* * *

Barbara Machann
Sedalia, Colorado
May 10, 2014

HAD I BEEN a homesteader bumping along in my covered wagon, searching for the perfect spot to start a new life out West, I would have stopped dead in my tracks on Barbara's land. On the bluff where her eleven-circuit labyrinth now sits, I would have built my house, where the vast beauty of lands meets sky.

"I usually don't answer my phone if I don't recognize the caller, but something told me to pick up when you called," Barbara smiled. "When you said the word labyrinth, there was no question. And you get two for the price of one! This is my friend, Mary."

Barbara and Mary led me, straightaway, along a gravel walkway to the backyard labyrinth. "We wanted you to see the labyrinth first thing!" Barbara said excitedly. "You can walk it now, if you'd like, then we can visit."

"Yes, I'd love to walk it," I replied, eager to anchor myself in a piece of this land that seemed to go on forever.

Mary joined me. "I like to sit in the center and absorb the peacefulness," she remarked quietly, as we stepped into the center minutes apart. I eased onto the warm rocks beside her and we shared the silence.

Barbara and glasses of ice water waited for us under the shade of an umbrella in her backyard garden. "Mary has been such a blessing these last two years," she said. "I had a hip replacement in 2012 and was fussing around, wondering how I was going to keep up the labyrinth. The weeds would have taken over if she hadn't come along."

"I tell people that Barbara birthed the labyrinth and I adopted it," Mary laughed. "The way it happened is so strange. My husband and I thought we were going to another labyrinth in Sedalia, where his meditation class was meeting. We looked it up on the Labyrinth Locator, found the address for Barbara's, by mistake, and came here."

"They walked up to my garage and asked about the meeting. Of course, there was no meeting here, but that was just when I needed help with the labyrinth. Mary volunteered and has been coming ever since. We've made a connection that I could have never imagined."

Mary nodded, "We're sisters."

"Soul sisters," Barbara added.

"I knew about labyrinths for quite a while before I met Barbara," Mary said. "I'd even put it on my bucket list to build one someday but didn't have enough space. Walking has been incredibly healing for me, especially after I was diagnosed with breast cancer. One day I was so overwhelmed that I rushed out the door and started walking. I thought, 'I can survive this, if I walk.' And labyrinths kept popping up in different places."

"I've been around a few more years than Mary, so I knew about labyrinths back in the '90s. The first one I walked was at the University of Denver in 1998 after I read about it in the paper. I said, 'I've got to go walk it,' and I did. Then I bought every book I could find about them, which wasn't much. But we're not drawn to labyrinths as a mental exercise. We come to them through our hearts and feelings.

"After that first walk," Barbara continued, "I felt completely at peace and got the idea to build my own. But first I had to collect rocks to line the path. That took a while because I only selected rocks that spoke to me.

"Then when I tried to put them in place," she went on, "I realized that it was the rocks, not me, that were deciding where to go. I'd lay one on the path and it might say, 'No, not here.' So I'd pick it up and find one that would say, 'Yes, right here.' I placed every rock that way.

"And look at this," Barbara said, gesturing for us to follow her to the labyrinth. "Do you notice a piece of marble in every single row? I didn't do that by design; the Universe did. It came together beautifully."

Barbara approached the edge of the bluff where the ground began its steady course downward toward Plum Creek. "Sometimes I'll walk down to those trees where there's a meditation spot and just listen. I love this land. It talks to me."

"There are treasures tucked all over this place," Mary said, linking her arm through Barbara's.

I remembered a comment Mary had made as we walked out of the labyrinth earlier that afternoon. "When Barbara told me you were coming, I thought. 'This woman doesn't know what treats she's in for.' "

I knew. I was looking at them.

EN ROUTE

Denver, Colorado
Hotel
May 10, 2014
Mother's Day Flowers, Part 2

BARBARA ASKED ME to stay for lunch. She had set the table while Mary and I were walking the labyrinth. I admired her delicate teacups, water goblets and silky tablecloth decorated with pink blossoms. Blossoms … my roses! I had almost forgotten them in the car.

"I'll be right back," I said, rushing out the front door.

They were waiting patiently in their box on the floorboard. Not one had dropped her head in discouragement or fatigue. None complained of the stuffy car. Such strong spirits. I would miss these traveling companions.

They deserved a proper home with another woman, perhaps a mother, who would appreciate the love that sent them. Barbara, a mother and grandmother, was the perfect choice.

I returned to the house carrying the vase and relayed the flowers' story to Barbara and Mary—from delivery, to Cheyenne, to Denver, and now to Sedalia. I paraphrased Drew's note then we all wiped our tears on Barbara's floral napkins.

The roses became the honored guests, sitting proudly between Barbara and Mary. They didn't contribute to the conversation, but I could tell from their expressions that they were pleased.

When it was time to leave, I hugged Mary then Barbara and waved goodbye to the roses.

"Drive carefully," I imagined them saying. "And, Twylla, watch that speed limit."

I LEFT ALL the roses, except one, with Barbara. Wanting to be fair to all eighteen, I closed my eyes and selected a single stem. With every petal intact, she survived the remainder of the trip layered in a zippered bag, inside a shoe, under a pair of neatly folded jeans in my suitcase. Now dried, she stands upright in a blue glass vase on my writing desk. She's been particularly helpful as I've written this story.

Cherylee Brewer
Pinedale, Arizona
May 11, 2014

A DAY OF extremes! De-icing in Denver. High wind warnings in Albuquerque. Gusts that threatened to sweep my compact rental car off I-40, gradually calmed as I turned south toward Pinedale. Finally, only a warm afternoon breeze remained as I parked in front of

Cherylee's house mid-afternoon.

"What a trip you've had today!" Cherylee exclaimed. "And Happy Mother's Day, by the way."

She offered me a glass of water and introduced me to her husband, Kent, and daughter, Terrylee. We all followed her into the living room where she invited me to sit beside her on the couch. It felt refreshing to sit anywhere that didn't have a steering wheel in front of it.

"Happy Mother's Day to you, too." I replied. The Labyrinth Locator lists your whole family as the builders, so I'm thinking that you have other children."

"Six all together. We had Terrylee first, then adopted five Russian children, ages nine to seventeen, in 2001. They all pitched in to build the labyrinth, hauling rocks mainly."

Kent nodded. "I remember asking Cherylee, 'So where do you want these rocks?' She would refer to her instructions and tell us to place them here and there. As we went along, we had to reposition them because the labyrinth got scrunched in the corner of the property."

"Then the entrance didn't come together like the picture," Cherylee added. "But we finally got it done, all in one afternoon. Our neighbors would drive by, look and wonder, 'What in the world are they doing?'

"I'd actually been thinking about building one for a while, ever since our friend, Dennis, showed me a picture. I was drawn to it. Then one Sunday afternoon I just announced to the family, 'We're going to build a labyrinth today!' It turned out to be a bonding time for us. We've even developed rituals when we walk it like waiting until everyone is in the center, then giving group hugs."

"And touching hands as we pass each other," Terrylee said, then added with a laugh, "The older kids used to tease me that the devil was going to get me if I crossed a line."

Cherylee smiled at her daughter then continued in a more serious tone. "I didn't know what to expect, what the labyrinth was going to do. But somehow I just knew that we needed it. When we built it, we were experiencing a huge trauma in our lives, a journey of transition. I was homeschooling the kids. Our Russian children had learning challenges and attachment issues. I started having them walk the labyrinth before school or when they got stuck, needed to cool off, relax, or get at peace. They would return calmer."

"It was a purposeful dedication of our property, part of the process of attaching to a lot of different healing tools," Kent explained. "That's when we started our biodynamic gardening beds and sharing food with others as ways to bring harmony into the world."

Seconds passed in silence. I noticed that the wind had picked up as limbs in the front yard arched further toward the ground.

"Looking back, our journey really changed after we built the labyrinth," Cherylee reflected. "It's been a spiritual journey toward health in so many facets of our lives."

She reached for her jacket. "Terrylee and I thought you might like to walk the labyrinth with us on Mother's Day."

Acts of kindness continued to touch my life when I least expected them, or rather when I didn't expect them at all. Therein lies their beauty.

"Thank you, it would be my pleasure!" I answered.

Terrylee extended her hand as we passed on the path, in the family tradition. We continued to walk and touch hands until we met Cherylee in the center and hugged.

"This labyrinth has been my friend through some of the biggest challenges and changes in my life," Cherylee said, before we began the return journey. "It was my place to come for some peace, serenity and centering. Now that I'm older, my walks are more purposeful like for prayer and meditation. Sometimes I'll walk at sunrise or sunset and face the four directions."

Kent met us at the entrance with a ladder for my photoshoot.

"We love rocks," he said, "and the labyrinth is a way for us to honor the unique ones in this area. I found this little white one yesterday at the old Pinedale school lot where my great-grandmother used to play. I placed it in the labyrinth as a memory."

I was repositioning the ladder to accommodate for lengthening shadows when Vladimir, one of Cherylee and Kent's sons, joined us. The timing was perfect for one more photo … of the labyrinth with its family.

EN ROUTE

Show Low, Arizona
Hotel
May 11, 2014

TWENTY MINUTES AFTER leaving Cherylee's house, I arrived in the hotel lobby. I saw the sign at once. A large, rectangular white board scripted in red letters announced:

Welcome, Ms. Alexander!
You are the Guest of the Day!

Surely there was another Ms. Alexander. How could I be the Guest of the Day? I hadn't signed up for a drawing, wasn't a Platinum, Silver, Diamond or any other kind of mega points member.

"So, uh, I'm Twylla Alexander," I haltingly informed the hotel clerk. But I may not be *the* Ms. Alexander on your sign."

"Of course! Ms. Alexander. We've got your suite all ready."

"My suite? How did this happen?"

"We randomly select a guest every day to be upgraded. You're the lucky one today!"

Why did I think there was still a catch?

She handed me a card key and pointed me to the elevator.

So, there I was on a comfy couch in a HUGE suite complete with queen bed, kitchen and private balcony. Best of all, there was a basket of treats: peanuts, crackers, popcorn, Oreos. My dinner!

A handwritten card peeked out behind the popcorn:

Ms. Alexander. We hope you have a pleasant stay.
The Staff of the Show Low Hampton Inn

Another act of kindness.

Liz Paterson
Cerrillos, New Mexico
May 12, 2014

THE SAME ROAD I drove yesterday felt like undiscovered territory today, all five hours of it, back to Albuquerque. The wind that consumed my attention had obviously whooshed on down the road, gratefully taking ninety percent of the truck traffic with it.

My GPS directed me to abandon asphalt for dirt as I neared Liz's address. Jolting along a road that felt more like a gully, I stopped at an adobe-style house that fit the description in her email.

"Liz?" I asked the woman who answered the door.

"No, that's my mother, the lady waving from the *casita* down the hill."

Since I had no idea what a casita was, I looked for the woman. Spotting her, I turned the car around and jolted in her direction.

"I'm so proud of you!" Liz exclaimed, hugging me. "You found it! If you kept going along that road, you'd come to the labyrinth, close to the *arroyo*."

Another unfamiliar word.

"A dry creek or riverbed. I'll show it all to you when we walk down there later."

We sat at Liz's kitchen table, separated from the desert by a sliding glass door. She followed my gaze to the magical landscape she experienced every day.

"There's something about this place. You feel so connected to the planet here. It's too scary for some people, though, too barren and windy. There's no place to hide. My husband and I adore it."

The wind, I knew about.

"We have a granddaughter who lives in New York City, like you. When she comes here, I take her for rides in the sidecar of my motorcycle. When she leaves, she feels great. Something here just opens people up."

"Ok, Liz," I said spontaneously. "I have to ask because I think it's super inspiring that you ride a motorcycle. How old are you?"

"Seventy-four!" she said, without as much as a half-second pause.

"Amazing!" I shouted amidst our wild applause and laughter.

"Instead of sitting here, let's walk on down to the labyrinth," she said.

I'd try to match her pace.

"After I discovered labyrinths, I knew I wanted to build one in this valley. I call it the valley, but it's a canyon really," Liz explained as we reached the bottom of the road. "There's such a feeling of safety and calmness here. We actually found shells when we built the labyrinth because there was an ocean here at least three times, a huge ocean. When it receded, it formed all these canyons as it rushed out to Mother Sea.

"Can you feel that it's a woman's space?" Liz asked. "Not that I tell men they can't enter, but once they see all the goddess figures, they get it."

She crossed over the labyrinth lines to the far edge and touched the uplifted arms of a woman's clay torso. "I made her. Her arms feel more like wings now, and she's pregnant. She's the total, happy guardian of the labyrinth. I just love her!

"Almost everything you see in the labyrinth, except for the large pieces of glass, has been left by women. I've facilitated workshops for women from all over the country. They bring their tents and camp out down here. We do goddess work. Women need support and nurturing. We are the ones who need to take the reins of this world and change things.

"And I have a ceremony for women around Halloween," she continued, "when we bring food from our grandmothers' recipes. We set it around a fire and share a great meal as we tell stories about our mothers, sisters, grandmothers and great-grandmothers. The stories are for them, to keep them alive.

"Would you like to walk the labyrinth with me?" she asked. "If you need some quiet time first, you can sit on this bench behind my Pause Rock."

Pause Rock. I liked that name and what it implied, but I was ready to join Liz. I'd search for a smaller version to slip in my pocket as I circled the labyrinth.

"I tell women that they may want to ask a question as they walk in, then let it go when they get to the center. Letting their minds be as free as possible on the way out allows answers to enter. The answers are already inside us, though, sent down to us from our mothers and grandmothers, from all those who have come before."

As I stepped onto the sandy path, the same question surfaced that has traveled with me for almost two years.

"How is this journey changing me?" The labyrinth has never answered. I've never expected it to. It keeps me company as I discern the answers for myself.

Answers, as Liz said, that are already within me.

17

Quietude

Nebraska

Sister Marie Andre Shon, Nebraska.

~ Twylla's journal ~

Chicago Midway Airport
Layover on flight from Newark to Omaha
June 4, 2014

THREE STATES REMAIN, three women to meet, three labyrinths to walk.

Each will be a single-state visit: Nebraska, Louisiana then Hawaii. I'm on my own until Hawaii, when Marian joins me for number fifty.

I remember when she and I had *visited* only three—Rhode Island, New Hampshire and Maine—and forty-seven remained. But I've never visualized this journey in terms of how many states were left, like a daunting rock formation on the far horizon. It's always been about the next state, the next woman—one visit at a time.

As I draw closer to the end of this fifty-state journey, the inklings of reflection crowd closer and closer into my consciousness. Questions wait patiently for answers:

How has this journey changed me?
What have I learned?
How have the lives of almost fifty women impacted my own?

But I continue to keep them at bay. I'm not yet ready for the depth of reflection that a journey's end invites. I imagine a day or days when my journal and I will spend time together somewhere beside a labyrinth— a *high tree day*, a friend once termed it. Time for perspective when you're up above the fray. A time of intention.

But today is not that day.

Instead, it's time for a bathroom stop, a cup of tea and snack for the plane, then the next visit—with Sister Marie Andre.

* * *

Sister Marie Andre Shon
Missionary Benedictine Sisters
Immaculata Monastery and Spirituality Center
Norfolk, Nebraska
June 4, 2014

ONCE AGAIN, I dodged severe weather by one day, as evidenced by uprooted trees and downed power lines strewn along the route from the airport. Sunshine filtered through leaves still dripping with yesterday's rain. The monastery's calm presence felt like a welcoming haven.

"We thought you might not come after the storms we had yesterday," Sister Marie Andre said, shaking my hand. "A tornado touched down close by and we had much hail."

She gestured toward a chair at the end of a long conference table. "Please sit here. I'll ask one of the sisters to bring you a glass of water.

"I'm not quite sure where to begin to tell you about the labyrinth," she stated with a smile that appeared as much in her eyes as on her lips.

"I'd like to hear your story, about how the labyrinth came into your life," I answered.

"I grew up in Korea where there are many formations of labyrinths, but I didn't know what they were. I did not walk one until 1999. I came to the monastery in 1982, thirty-two years ago and received a sabbatical in '98. I went to England to study. In one of our classes we were encouraged to write poetry and draw. I kept drawing circles, multi-layered circles and spirals. I logically interpreted that to mean that I had accumulated stifled energies that needed to be untangled.

"Then during one of the weekends," Sister Marie Andre continued, "we went to France and happened to stop at Chartres Cathedral. By God's grace, the labyrinth was open that day for walkers. Something pulled me into that circle. Immediately, I felt a *coming-home* sensation. I kind of lost myself and was transported elsewhere; but because my group was hurrying to see other places, we had to leave.

"After that, I began researching information about labyrinths. I came back to my monastic community in '99 and wanted to build one on the grounds, but I had to wait. Labyrinths were foreign to the community, so I introduced them bit by bit. Everybody journeys in different stages and you can't force anything."

A sister entered and placed a glass of water and a small plate of cookies on the table.

"You asked if I designed our labyrinth, but I can't say that I did since the labyrinth has been around for three thousand years or so," Sister Marie Andre laughed. "But I did modify it. We kept the eleven-circuit Chartres design, but enlarged it from 42.3 feet to 57 feet to fit the space more harmoniously. I also chose the location, materials, and arranged the surrounding environment. We were so blessed to have Paul, the director of our physical plant, and his team. He is really a saintly person. He had never heard of a labyrinth, but successfully followed my attempts at explanation. And I'm kind of a particular person, I'll have to admit."

Paul happened to be in his office when Sister Marie Andre and I dropped by a few minutes later. He joined us at the labyrinth.

"Sister Marie Andre had the vision and we built it. From start to finish, it took about six months. The flagstones for the path came from Colorado and I needed to break them up and fit them together like a puzzle."

"And I wanted grass between the stones like an organic life,"

Sister Marie Andre added. "I designed the entrance facing south, right off the sidewalk so people can access it freely from the street."

As she said that, I realized what was missing from the labyrinth. There were no signs of religious affiliation, no crosses, angels, statues, no Biblical inscriptions on plaques. I shared my observation with her.

"The labyrinth is a universal design," Sister Marie Andre explained. "It's for our neighbors, the community—anybody—to walk, without having to even come through our front gate. I really wanted to build it on our grounds because there's a human wisdom and instinct that enables people to communicate with the sacred being or energy, even if they don't use the word God. The labyrinth is a special form of blessing for all who walk it."

For the next half hour, Sister Marie Andre and I silently followed the stone path, which was adorned only by a simple circle of oak trees. An outdoor church, a sacred space, an ancient design—no label was needed. The blessing was the same.

EN ROUTE

Omaha, Nebraska
Hotel
June 4, 2014

I DIDN'T LEAVE Immaculata Monastery immediately following the labyrinth walk. I stayed for three more hours at Sister Marie Andre's invitation. I had already taken up two hours of her time and assumed she had other commitments. But even if she did, she focused her complete attention on me, her guest. Sister Gemma Peters had treated me in the same gracious manner when I visited the Benedictine Sisters of Annunciation in Bismarck, North Dakota.

"Would you like a tour of the monastery?" she asked.

"If it's not too much trouble," I answered, still concerned that I was imposing on her time, although I was clearly the only anxious one in the room.

Sister Marie Andre guided me through all aspects of the sisters' lives—the chapel, dining room, sun porch, craft rooms, laundry, infirmary and hallways that led to their private quarters. Each room was orderly, all supplies in place. Furniture and floors were uncluttered.

The sisters moved through their day within a framework of structure and calm, from worship to work, nourishment to contemplation. Their voices and actions created a steady rhythm that my own body began to imitate and my spirit began to savor.

I remembered when I had first been drawn to a contemplative life. Reading Kathleen Norris' book *The Cloister Walk*, Thomas Merton's autobiography*The Seven Storey Mountain*, and Nora Gallagher's *Things Seen and Unseen: A Year Lived in Faith.* I wondered how I might incorporate intentional, reflective practices into my daily life. Thich Nhat Hanh's *Peace Is Every Step* became my gateway to mindfulness teachings and meditation.

Perhaps Sister Marie Andre sensed my reflective mood when she offered another invitation.

"We would be pleased to have you join us for Vespers at 5:00, followed by a simple monastic meal. The other sisters will be eating in silence, but there is a separate room where you and I could eat."

Of course, I would stay.

Sister Marie Andre had already prepared a place for me in the pew beside her. She had marked pages in the prayerbook so I could keep up. At dinner, she offered me the first helping of ham, rice and broccoli casserole, salad and grapes. She listened while I talked, then cleared the dishes.

She walked me to the car and hugged me.

"As we walked the labyrinth," she said, "I thought, 'Here is a beautiful soul who's on a journey of a higher level, perhaps a journey to her Self.'"

A journey to my Self ....
How did she know?

18

Beginnings and Endings

Louisiana

Michele Fry, Louisiana.

~ Twylla's journal ~

Bed and Breakfast
Natchitoches, Louisiana
June 12, 2014

I've never known exactly how to pronounce Natchitoches so I paid close attention to Kathy, the owner of the B&B when she checked me in this afternoon.

"*Nak-a-dish*," she said, with heavy emphasis on "*nak*," before almost swallowing the last two syllables. It would take considerable practice before I could sound like a local.

I arrived at 4:00, after driving three hours from Michele Fry's labyrinth in Baton Rouge. I could have driven six and a half hours straight back to our home in Arkansas, but there's one more detour I want to make before this journey is over. That will come tomorrow, but this evening I'm pretending to be the fashionable lady of this two-story Victorian home (circa 1895). Unbelievably, I'm the only guest.

"We're booked for tomorrow night, but tonight it's all yours," Kathy mentioned when she gave me the key to my room, and the house.

I've stayed in traditional hotels on every trip for the last two years, but on this next-to-last visit, I'm treating myself. Sipping sparkling water out of a cut-glass goblet, I'm careful not to spill a single drop on the high-backed velvet love seat. Floor-to-ceiling windows, framed with tieback curtains, look out on a broad wraparound porch. Candles flicker in lanterns on the mantle.

Perhaps I'll select a book from the extensive selection in the library then climb the elegant, curved staircase to my room with its four-poster bed and fireplace; or settle into a rocking chair on the porch and watch the world go by; or indulge in one (or two) of Kathy's homemade oatmeal raisin cookies.

I wonder which choice the real lady of the house might make on an evening all to herself.

Surely, the same as I.

All three!

Michele Fry
Baton Rouge, Louisiana
June 12, 2014

Michele Fry and John Nagle, "The Labyrinth Tenders."

Their title on the Labyrinth Locator sounded like a profession, a person whose job it is to take care of labyrinths like a doctor who makes house calls. Their own grass labyrinth, a seventy-foot Chartres design, appeared perfectly sculpted on the Locator photo.

In person, it looked ... different.

"We may not be the best people to talk to," Michele said as our conversation began. "The labyrinth isn't my priority like it used to be. A couple of years ago I said to John, 'Let's just let it grow over. We don't really use it that much.' "

"But I said," John quickly added, "We've got to keep it. Every time I enter it or mow it, or just walk across the yard, I acknowledge it in my mind. It's automatic."

"Don't get me wrong," Michele went on, "The labyrinth has been a wonderful experience for me as a builder and tender. I used to walk it and imagine that I was in a crystal dome. Everything went away except me and the labyrinth. But now when I go out there, all I notice is that the weeds need mowing, the fountain doesn't work, the bridges are rotten. It feels like a chore; whereas before, it was hard work but it was a joy."

This was the first time I had heard a woman speak of her labyrinth in less than a positive light. I appreciated Michele's honesty but didn't know how to respond. So I listened.

"I like to live on a high plane of enthusiasm," Michele explained. "My mother's in an assisted living facility and I go visit her every other day. It's so compelling to be helpful and useful there. And I help people find their lost pets since I lost my dog, Lucky Lucy. The labyrinth has gone to the side."

John leaned forward in his chair beside Michele on the front porch. "For years we were totally involved in building labyrinths in Baton Rouge. People call us the grandmother and grandfather of labyrinths here. There was only one other labyrinth in the city when we built ours fifteen years ago. We became members of the Baton Rouge Labyrinth Society. We painted labyrinths on canvas and built brick ones in parks. We mowed them and maintained them."

Michele nodded. "We helped organize candlelight walks, Martin Luther King Day walks and more. It was all very exciting. But after a time, the society split up. I loved being part of a team. I've missed those connections."

"We should tell her about how the labyrinth brought us together," John smiled.

"Of course! That was when we barely knew each other and decided to go walk a seven-circuit labyrinth together. We both focused our eyes on the path, trying to have a spiritual experience. Then I heard this booming voice in my head say, 'He's the one!' Now, I was loving my independence as a confirmed bachelorette after two divorces."

John picked up the story. "And I'd been divorced twice but wanted a relationship. When we met at the end of the walk, I shared with her that I'd heard a voice that said, 'She's the one!' "

"So, here we are!" Michele exclaimed, grinning at John.

"We had hoped that our labyrinth would be more of a connector," he said. "We offered it to the public as a community service but not as many people came to walk it."

"A few church groups came, which was our vision," Michele added. "We've had plenty of events for family and friends in the labyrinth like New Year's Eve parties, but the one thing it's missing is people walking it, regularly. That's another reason why my interest in it has waned."

John held up a glossy color photograph of the labyrinth in its perfectly sculpted condition. "We can use this as a guide when we walk it," he suggested. "Portions of the path have faded and the edges aren't as distinct as they used to be."

I trailed closely behind Michele and John, who needed to consult the photograph only once. Although a bit weary and dotted with mud puddles from a recent rain, the path remained walkable and seemed to enjoy our company.

"What will you do if you decide to close your labyrinth?" I asked.

Michele answered. "I would leave it just like it is. The pattern will stay for years, even if we don't do anything, because we maintained the design for so long. Like I said, we may not be the best people to talk to on your journey."

I disagreed. With one state remaining, endings were exactly what I needed to contemplate. Michele, John, the labyrinth and I were at similar places in our journeys.

EN ROUTE

Melrose Plantation
25 miles southeast of Natchitoches, Louisiana
June 13, 2014

THE PARKING LOT was empty. Melrose, a National Historic Landmark, didn't open for fifteen more minutes. The fields around the house lay quiet, the grove of pecan trees were still on a breezeless morning when humidity hung heavy. I pulled a book from my tote bag, the one that brought me here—*Art From Her Heart, Folk Artist Clementine Hunter*, by Kathy Whitehead and illustrated by Shane W. Evans. A children's book.

I had never heard of Clementine Hunter before I walked into the children's section of the Harlem library last February. It was Black History Month, and books about African-Americans were prominently displayed on the tops of bookshelves and spread out on low tables. Clementine seemed to be staring directly at me from her central position on the cover, inviting me to read her story. So I did.

Squeezing into a child-size chair, I opened to the first page:

> "Clementine waited until her work in the Big House was done and the twinkle of stars filled the night sky above the Cane River. She was ready to paint, like the artists she cooked and cleaned for on Melrose Plantation."

Page after page, I was swept into her story.

A "free black," whose days of physical labor on Melrose were spent much like her Grandmother Idole's, a slave.

A self-taught artist who stole moments whenever she could to paint—on window shades, bottles, roofing shingles, and cardboard—with leftover paints and brushes.

A woman who displayed her art on a clothesline and charged twenty-five cents admission for people to look, and who lived to see her paintings eventually sell for hundreds of thousands of dollars.

What was it about Clementine's story that captivated me so intensely that I added an extra day and over a hundred miles to this trip?

The author captures it in her repeated refrains:

> "When Clementine decided to paint pictures, she didn't wait for the perfect art studio."
>
> "She didn't wait to travel and seek inspiration in foreign lands."
>
> "Clementine didn't wait for the world to find her art."

Clementine didn't wait. She painted because it was in her to do it. And she found a way to make it happen.

I came to see her original paintings.

I came to celebrate her creative, "can-do" spirit on the land where she lived all her 102 years.

I came … because I wanted to capture some of that spirit for myself.

19

Full Circle

Hawaii

Eve Hogan, Hawaii.

~ Twylla's journal ~

35,000 feet above the Pacific Ocean
July 2, 2014

"Our last trip could be Hawaii," I remember Marian saying somewhere on a road in Pennsylvania, forty-one states ago.

"Yes!" I answered enthusiastically. "All four of us—you, Jim, Drew and I—could go and rent a condo for a whole week."

"Surely there's a woman in Hawaii who's built her own outdoor labyrinth," Marian said. "You'll just have to find her."

I was confident that I could. For two years, I've imagined this unknown woman standing beside a labyrinth among lush, tropical plants welcoming me. Tomorrow morning at 10 a.m., Eve Hogan and her labyrinth at Sacred Garden Maui will become real to me.

Drew and I will land in three hours. I reach across the aisle and squeeze the hand of my Unwavering Supporter. Not once has he as much as rolled his eyes at this journey, asked how much it's costing, questioned my ability, sanity or purpose. Quite the opposite. He has actively encouraged me. And he sent me eighteen long-stemmed roses when I was in Denver on Mother's Day!

A journey is possible, I suppose, without that kind of support. But the path would be tilted, uphill.

Eve Hogan
Makawao, Maui, Hawaii
July 3, 2014

It was just as I imagined: a labyrinth framed by dense, tropical growth that protected rather than consumed it; a shared space held by design and nature; a welcoming presence to four visitors who had come a distance.

Eve invited us to sit with her in the Buddha Garden before we walked the labyrinth. "He's huge, isn't he?" she asked. "Five feet tall and four feet wide, carved entirely out of one piece of wood. It's Buddha's sweet, peaceful face that attracted me to him. He's overheard me tell my labyrinth story many times, but never lets on.

"Someone gave me a copy of Lauren Artress's book *Walking a Sacred Path* about twenty years ago," Eve began, "and I loved the title. There was a picture of a labyrinth on the cover but I didn't know what it was. As soon as I opened it, I fell in love with the concept. It was a perfect experiential tool for people to practice skills I was already teaching, what I call "The Essential Life Skills." I went to Grace Cathedral for my facilitator training then came back here and immediately bought a canvas labyrinth.

"You should have seen me carting it around," Eve laughed. "It weighed about a hundred pounds. It got moldy in this climate so I'd bleach it, then have to wait for it to dry before I could use it again. When my husband and I started looking for places to live, I'd scope out the grounds for just the spot to build a labyrinth."

Eve pointed toward the path leading to the labyrinth as she continued. "At the time we bought this property, that was a pathway to nowhere—some people might think—just a clear space, circled by Kukui trees. But I knew. It was perfect for a labyrinth, truly a divinely thought-of space.

"Follow me. I'll show you!" she exclaimed.

We bid Buddha *aloha,* although he hardly seemed to notice, intent as he was on the delicate yellow hibiscus blossom in his hands.

"This is the second labyrinth we built here after the stream flooded and washed out the first. I tried to build the first one by myself; but after a couple of days of heavy lifting, I exclaimed, 'This is not my *kuleana,*' my 'responsibility or gift' in Hawaiian. So I said, 'Look, God, if you want a labyrinth here, you've got to help me figure out how to do it.'

"I kid you not," she continued excitedly. "That same day, two young men walked through the front door calling themselves *divine landscapers*. Well, that's what a labyrinth is, a divine landscape, so I hired them. Within a week, they had hauled the rocks in place and spread the gravel path. It was beautiful, with a heart-shaped center.

Eve moved a few feet past the labyrinth and pointed to a leisurely flowing stream.

"When the flood came, this stream went wild and totally overran the labyrinth. My first reaction was devastation. The time and money to rebuild was daunting. But I began to see the metaphor in it like a 180-degree turn on the labyrinth. I reframed the devastation and envisioned my labyrinth flowing out into the world. I came to embrace it. With just one mention of the labyrinth's loss on my Facebook page, people from all over the world sent money—over twenty thousand dollars. And people throughout the community pitched in to clear and rebuild in just one week! It was such an honoring, beautiful experience."

Six round stones formed the labyrinth's center, corresponding to the six petals of the rosette in the middle of the Chartres design. Marian, Jim, Drew, and I each selected one with Eve joining us on the fifth.

"I, personally, come to the labyrinth to be peaceful and present," Eve shared. "And it's a blessing to create a space, the labyrinth and garden, where the work continues whether I'm here or not. My work is all about creating relationships—healthy, harmonious relationships—with Self, Spirit and others."

She turned to me and continued, "Twylla, you have shared labyrinth walks and experienced relationships with so many people on your journey. I'm honored to be a part of this fiftieth walk."

Eve led us back to the entrance and asked me to begin. Before I could start, however, there was something I needed to get from my purse ... an 8.5 x 11-inch replica of the U.S. map, which had hung on my closet door for two years. Taped onto each state was the face of the woman whose labyrinth I had visited. Eve's photo would soon join them. In a symbolic way, they would finish the final walk with me.

I was ready.

~ from Twylla's journal ~

Oneloa Beach, Kapalua
Maui
July 4, 2014

Marian and Jim are beach people. They love the waves and sand. Marian's out there now with a boogie board. How old is she, anyway?

Considering it's the Fourth of July, the beach is relatively calm. Three or four families splash at water's edge. Children build sandcastles. Adults work on their tans. Dare-devil youths scream from distant rocks as they fling themselves into the ocean.

I'm still processing yesterday's labyrinth walk. Part of me expected fireworks, bells and thunderous applause would erupt in my head, that I would jump up and down or run the path. But the vast majority of me knew that it would be a quiet, meditative walk, the kind that nurtures my spirit, like a warm conversation with a good friend.

Memories from the day flow faster than I can write …

Emotions of gratitude and relief
Hugs from husband and friends
Words —
"I'm so proud of you."
"I can't believe you finished this journey in two years."
"Such an accomplishment."
"I love you."
Tears, theirs and my own

EVE QUIETLY LIT torches around the outer ring. She invited us to join her in the center where she struck a match to a bundle of white sage—for cleansing, wisdom and clarity. She circled our bodies, allowing the smoke to surround and enter.

With the power of ritual, Eve marked my fiftieth and final visit.

She blessed the women who had said yes, who had opened themselves and their labyrinths to my journey.

She spoke of Drew's constant support, encouragement and love.

She gave gratitude to Marian for her friendship and her enthusiasm, when my idea was only minutes old.

She thanked other friends (Margie, Mary, Geri) who traveled miles of the journey with me.

She recognized the close of my physical journey and the continuation of my writing.

Her final words were for me, only, after the sage was set aside and the torches extinguished.

"You know," she began, "the labyrinth called you to take this journey and write this book."

Before those words had a chance to register, she asked, "What have you learned?"

I'm not ready for that question, I thought. There's not just one answer, and I must have time to reflect, to write and cross out, to take in and own all I have experienced.

"What comes to your mind *first*?" Eve prompted. "You can always change or add as you reflect longer."

I looked down at my feet—still on the labyrinth—and said, "I followed my own path. I listened to my own voice."

"Let that become your affirmation as you walk out of the labyrinth," Eve said, offering a mantra for me to repeat:

I listen to my Self.
I honor my Self.
I continue the journey to my Self.

* * *

My High Tree Day will come with its hours of reflection when I'll ponder the lessons learned. I'll take notice of what fired my imagination, to what said, "Pay attention!" I'll celebrate the bridges crossed, the wind storms weathered. I'll cry, once more, for the women I met who died too soon. I'll remember all fifty with deepest gratitude and inspiration.

Perhaps I'll discover that after hours of reflection, I will answer Eve's question …exactly the same.

"Twylla, show me how to draw a labyrinth in the sand."

Marian's request jars me back to the present. I notice that the sun hovers closer to the horizon. Only one family remains at water's edge. The cliff divers have moved on to their next adventure.

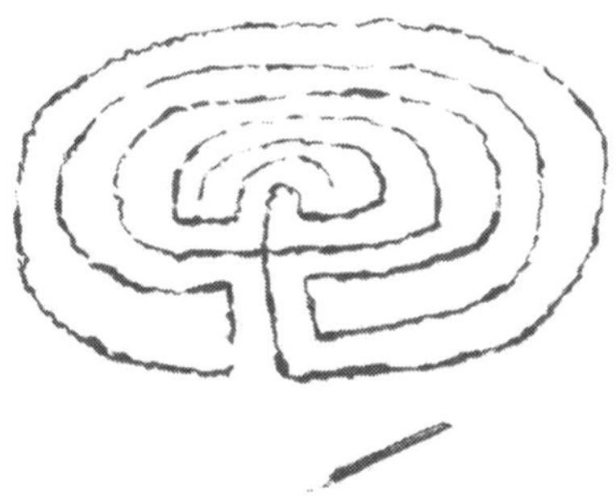

"Sure, be right there," I yell back over the crash of incoming waves.

Two years ago, I knelt beside Anne Hornstein on Miramar Beach in Florida on my first labyrinth visit. She picked up a stick and taught me how to draw a labyrinth in the sand, the first one I ever drew.

The journey has come full circle.

EN ROUTE

35,000 feet above the Pacific
July 9, 2014

Two fuschia bougainvillea petals tumbled out of my journal. I hurriedly plucked them from a bush outside our condo this morning as Drew loaded our suitcases in the car. Now flat and paper thin to the touch, they serve as tangible evidence that the magic of the past few days actually happened.

One story remains from my visit with Eve. Eve is not in the story, nor are any of the people I planned to be with me. The story's serendipity lies in the fact that it was not planned at all. When I began the journey two years ago, I expected the unexpected. It was through the unexpected that I envisioned the greatest opportunities for insight and personal growth.

I would have expected nothing less of the final encounter.

A YOUNG GIRL, around age ten, approached me as I walked away from Eve's labyrinth.

"Are you the lady who has visited a labyrinth in every state?" she asked.

Word sure gets around fast, I thought since I'd just this instant completed my final visit.

She had overheard Eve tell her mother about my journey as they toured the gardens.

"What is the favorite labyrinth that you visited?" she wondered.

I pulled the map from my purse and showed her the faces of all the women I had met.

"Each woman and labyrinth has such a special story, I couldn't pick a favorite. But if you'll select a state, I'll tell you the lady's story."

She chose California.

I described Mary Grove's Baltic Wheel labyrinth, the way it connects to the sidewalk in front of her house so neighbors and passers-by can enjoy it freely. I explained how Mary can no longer walk her labyrinth because of illness but enjoys watching others walk it from her dining room window.

She smiled and said, "That's nice."

"Can I take a picture of us together in the center of the labyrinth?" I asked, wanting to remember this much younger woman who shared an interest in labyrinths, journeys, or both.

"Standing or meditating?" she said, quite seriously. "My mother is a meditation teacher, and sometimes we meditate in the labyrinth."

I was touched by her gentle spirit and inquisitive nature, by such a young voice already expressing what interested her and acting on it.

We situated ourselves in a cross-legged position across from one another on stepping stones in the center, hands resting on our knees, eyes closed. For five minutes, we sat in silence, punctuated only by the sound of Hawaiian birdsong. I opened my eyes first and gently tapped her knee.

As we walked to the edge of the labyrinth together, I instinctively placed my hand on her shoulder, bent over, and whispered. "Maybe one day, you'll take your own journey."

With one firm nod of her head, we both knew she was already on her way.

The little girl in me was throwing a party.

20

Reflections in a Cathedral

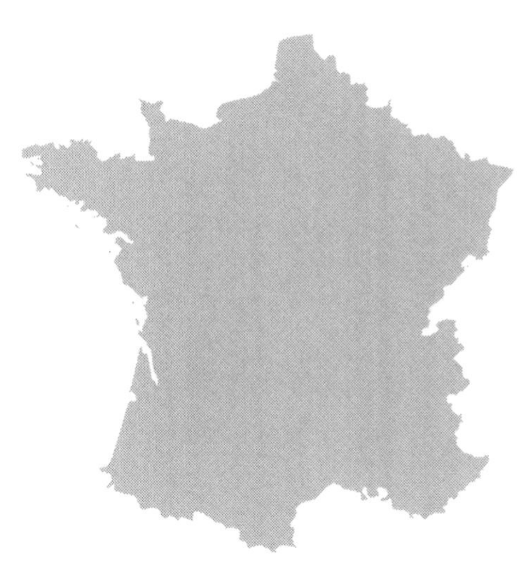

The author walking the labyrinth at Chartres Cathedral in France.

~Twylla's journal~

Chartres Cathedral, France
September 12–16, 2016

I ENTERED CHARTRES Cathedral for the first time and looked down rather than up at its Gothic grandeur, the opposite of everyone around me. My eyes searched the floor for the labyrinth, the 42.3-foot, eleven-circuit labyrinth created and constructed by master masons around the year 1200—the only surviving authentic medieval labyrinth. It lay directly ahead in the cathedral's nave, its center visible but the remainder covered by rows of wooden chairs, removed only on Fridays for walkers.

I selected a chair on the right-hand side directly over one of the labyrinth's turns and reverently placed my feet on its 800-year-old stone path. Visitors and worshipers passed me by, their voices a faint hum that got lost under the vastness of the vaulted ceilings. I paid them little notice as I tried to grasp the reality of my own presence in a space I had dreamed of visiting ever since I first heard the name *Chartres labyrinth.*

I had come to France to attend Lauren Artress's pilgrimage, "The Rising Phoenix: Birthing New Images in these Challenging Times," held for five days at Chartres. Since the Middle Ages, the cathedral has been the destination for thousands of pilgrims. The other participants and I were no exception as we traveled from many areas in the United States and three countries, on our own personal journeys.

For me, the trip to Chartres was meant to be a time for reflection. Two years had passed since I finished the fiftieth visit, during which time writing, editing, and rewriting had filled most of my days. I had spent little time pondering the question Eve Hogan had asked following my final labyrinth walk in Maui.

"What have you learned?"

Now that the writing was almost complete, the cathedral, and labyrinth, would provide the space and time I needed for discernment.

Over the next four days, I returned frequently to my spot in the cathedral. I closed my eyes, breathed calmly and allowed my thoughts to revisit my fifty-state journey. Women's faces, labyrinths, bridges, prairie grass, a chicken coop, cups of tea and conversation, rocks, planes, rental cars, companions—hundreds of images flooded my memory.

I saw the journey in sections, each a critical piece of the process; but what I needed to visualize was the whole, like the labyrinth without chairs. If I applied the big-picture perspective to my two years of travel, what larger discoveries might emerge?

Gradually, day by day, insights began to arise. I captured them here in my journal, sometimes writing in spurts before they had a chance to escape; at other times, doodling as the flow subsided. I share them as they came to me, in no order of priority or parallel sentence structure. It is but a start. Other epiphanies are already forging their way to the surface.

Women inspire me!

Each woman on this journey, for reasons uniquely her own, decided to build a labyrinth—not an easy task—in fact, quite challenging. Whether she needed to collect rocks, dig trenches, maneuver a Bobcat, push a lawnmower, or wait patiently for the land or her heart to show her the way, she persevered. She took action, from idea to completion, regardless if the work took a weekend or five years. And across all fifty states, the women's labyrinth stories and personal stories are intimately interconnected, both testaments to their strength, creativity, resilience and courage.

I need to be part of a community of women. I need to continue to listen to their stories and share my own. I need their unique perspectives and fresh insights, their validation and questions. I need their encouragement to grow and their support through the process. And I will be the same for them.

Fear is (more) manageable in tiny increments.

Even if I had recalled the adage, "Life by the inch is a cinch, by the yard is hard," as I gazed at the length of the Delaware Memorial Bridge or the ledge of Lost Trail Pass, the words would not have registered. I had to experience it for myself. I had to be the one clutching the steering wheel to realize that my way of coping with runaway fear is one car length at a time... one step, one breath at a time. That's not to say that the span of a bridge or a piece of disturbing news doesn't trigger a basketful of anxiety. But I now have a vision of myself succeeding, and I am good at repetition.

Suspend judgment.

I had never met a Seer or a Witch, never seen a Fairy Circle or heard of a labyrinth that served as a portal to star nations. I was unfamiliar with energy vortexes, devas (nature spirits) and dowsing with rods, prisms or thumb-checking. But when I encountered each of them in women's stories, I had a choice, a choice I had to make quickly. I could express skepticism or disbelief based on my limited knowledge and experience, or I could listen and learn. Choosing the later didn't mean that I didn't question, but that curiosity rather than judgment directed my actions. I was a welcomed guest in fifty women's homes. I left judgment at the door.

Follow nudges

I drove past the Castleton Free Library in Vermont. It beckoned me to stop and enter.

I did, and learned the meaning of my name.

I found a pine cone on Lisa's labyrinth in Alabama. It urged me to send it along to Karen whose labyrinth I had visited in Vermont.
I did, and Karen wrote that the pine cone brought her joy during her final months of hospice.

I noticed a pattern, after seven state visits, that I had unintentionally selected women's labyrinths. I felt that I should continue.
I did, and am now connected to an exceptional circle of women who continue to enrich my life.

Something encouraged me to detour from my prescribed route five times—at Gettysburg Battlefield, Springbank Retreat Center, Melrose Plantation, Knob Creek Farm, and Laura Ingalls' South Dakota prairie.
I did, and gained insight and inspiration from the land and the people who had passed there before me.

The same elusive something prompted me to reach out to the families of Karen, Patty, and Sarah, who died before the book was finished. I asked them to read the drafts of their loved ones' stories and provide feedback, as the other forty-seven women had done.
I did, and each family replied that it would be honored.

In each of these instances and more, I could have ignored the nudge, the gentle push that coaxed me to take action. But I didn't. And as Robert Frost observed in "The Road Not Taken," "that has made all the difference."

The person I've grown to accept as *Me* is open to revision.

Frequently during my two years of travel, I would picture myself from afar like an out-of-body experience with a video camera:

There I am, driving for six hours—alone—across the flat remoteness of North Dakota.

There I am, trying to decide whether to continue driving along I-40 in New Mexico in a turbulent windstorm or pull over and let it blow past.

There I am, getting out of a car somewhere in Ohio to write a poem about a wind turbine.

Who is that woman climbing into the back of a pickup truck in Idaho to take a photo of an extra-wide labyrinth? And the woman braking just in time to avoid a ditch while gaining a close-up view of sunflowers?

Me! But versions of Me that are only vaguely familiar, versions that are bolder, more confident, more spontaneous than ones I would readily recognize.

Yet, there they are. Images of Me—growing.

I must listen to and honor my own voice.

Votive candles lined the entire outer edge of the Chartres labyrinth the evening of our group's private walk. The rest of the cathedral disappeared into darkness. All the chairs had been removed and the complete design lay before me for the first time. Lauren stood at the entrance to the labyrinth motioning for each person to begin in turn. As I waited in line, I slipped off my shoes and socks. (We had been told that walking the labyrinth in bare feet was acceptable.) I wanted to sweep my soles over the cool stones and inch my toes into chips and along cracks. I wanted to physically touch the same space that other feet had trod for the past eight hundred years.

Yet seconds before, I hesitated to remove my shoes.

My voice said, "Of course! You've dreamed of walking the labyrinth with bare feet. Do it!"

A *competing* voice argued, "Walking without shoes is disrespectful, unladylike, New Age-y. Besides, your feet will get dirty."

Earlier in my life, when my voice was weaker, I might have listened to the preachy voice tinged with guilt and laden with shoulds;

but by the time Lauren touched my arm, my shoes and socks were off.

The tipping point? I knew that if I ignored my own dear voice, I would regret it—no, stronger than that—I would be heartbroken.

I stepped onto the labyrinth with joyful feet and a grateful heart. I embraced the dirt that turned the bottoms of my feet gray and triumphantly snapped a photo of them before I showered that night.

Eve's question, "What have you learned?" triggered a primal response free from excessive thought or cross-examination.

"I followed my own path. I listened to my own voice," I had answered, minutes after I completed the final walk of my journey.

As transformative as other lessons learned have been, the words I spoke to Eve that day have remained as the most empowering of all. I carry the affirmation she created for me on a piece of paper in my purse and have inscribed it forever in my memory. It shines forth on the final page of this book as a mantra and a reminder … that a journey ultimately leads to the Self.

And—like a labyrinth—it is a continuous path filled with endless possibilities.

I listen to my Self.
I honor my Self.
I continue the journey to my Self.

EPILOGUE

My Very Own Labyrinth

Greenbrier, Arkansas
July 23, 2014

ANNE HORNSTEIN, THE first woman I visited on my fifty-state journey, arrived from Florida to consecrate the space for my labyrinth. Knowing that I planned to begin work on it soon, she had called to offer her assistance with the consecration. I appreciated Anne's generous offer, but frankly the idea had never occurred to me.

"What exactly does that mean?" I asked.

"It's a ceremony, a way to bless and thank the land for embracing the labyrinth," she explained.

The idea of thanking the land resonated intuitively with me and although I wasn't sure what the ceremony would look like, I replied with enthusiasm. The labyrinth would begin its life in gratitude.

Anne stood in what would become the labyrinth's center and lit a bundle of white sage. "Sage cleanses, purifies and increases spiritual awareness," she said as smoke curled in ever-lengthening spirals over our heads.

Like a dancer, Anne flowed freely from the center to the outer edges of the labyrinth's space directing smoke to all areas. She thanked the land, trees, rocks, grass and all the animals that dwelled in or scampered over it. She blessed the spirit of J. B. (James Brown)—beloved family dog—who had been buried in the center, years before the labyrinth was even a long-awaited dream.

Finally, Anne fanned the sage's smoke around my body and thanked me for bringing the labyrinth to the land. She passed the smudge wand to me. My own emotions, coupled with the smoke's pungent fragrance, overpowered my own words of gratitude. So I simply smiled and bowed, deeply, in a continuous circle.

The land and I were ready.

Nine months later
April 11, 2015

I LOOKED OUT our bedroom window on the space below where the forty-two foot Chartres labyrinth would be created over the next two days. Our son, Jason, and son-in-law Ben were on their way with wheelbarrows, shovels and strong backs. Grandchildren Luke, Nate, Ruby and Anna, equipped with new pairs of work gloves, accompanied their dads.

Nine yards of topsoil, 115 rolls of Bermuda sod and 1,165 bricks lay in the front yard, ready.

The day had been a long time coming, much longer than I expected.

Two weeks after Anne left in July, I implemented Plan A. Ben helped me measure the pattern, dig the trench, and lay brick for the center and first concentric circle. I thought I could—and I wanted to—complete the remaining ten circles myself, one trench and one brick at a time. It would be a mindful meditation. I was in no hurry. I would work at my own pace, like I walk the labyrinth.

But then came the ninety-five degree afternoon in August when

I spent forty-five minutes unearthing two hulking rocks only to discover a network of entrenched tree roots underneath. I threw my shovel in the air, plopped down on the ground and reached for my phone.

"So, Ben, what was your plan again?" I asked our son-in-law who had tactfully suggested an alternative to my dig-a-trench method earlier in the planning process.

Without a hint of "I-told-you-so" in his voice, Ben outlined Plan B which I was, by then, more than happy to embrace.

"We need to wait until spring," Ben explained, "then the sod will have the best chance to take hold. We'll till the ground, shovel topsoil over it, mark the design, lay the bricks, then fit the sod to the path. It'll be a lot of work, but you, Jason, and I should be able to get it done in a couple of days, if we plan well and have all the materials in place."

I trusted Ben and knew that I needed help, but spring was two seasons away.

As was the case with so many of the women whose labyrinths I had visited, my own labyrinth was already creating opportunities for me ... opportunities to practice patience, to appreciate the contributions of a caring community, and to realize that Plan A isn't the only—or even the best—way.

* * *

After two full days of dirty, sweaty, intensely physical and joyful labor, Ben, Jason, and I (along with four little helpers) checked off the final step of Plan B.

The labyrinth was born!

Crickets had begun their evening chatter by the time everyone left. The labyrinth and I were alone to get acquainted. I couldn't walk on the sod for at least a week to allow time for the roots to get established, so I sat on the ground beside it. I patted the freshly laid path and whispered, "Hello, dear labyrinth."

Two months later
June 27, 2015

Pink and white petunias in a basket hung from a Shepherd's hook near the labyrinth's entrance. A pair of rock cairns—formed by stacks of three rocks from our yard topped by a chunk of Arkansas quartz—marked the opening. The quartz were gifts from grandsons Luke and Nate. Luke had said, "Grandmom, this is for your labyrinth."

Two concrete benches flanked the labyrinth's north and south sides under thick coverings of oak leaves. A pot of Angel Wing red begonias sat at the feet of each, ready to welcome the guests who would be arriving shortly.

I knew midway through my travels that I would dedicate my labyrinth when it was finished. The idea sprang from women along the way who had dedicated their labyrinths, declaring them special places, sacred places, and places of peace. I added the word celebration to dedication as a reason to gather people around my beautiful, new labyrinth.

I sent invitations to the fifty women and to my family and friends. I had no idea how many of the women might attend, but I wanted them to know that they were welcome in body or spirit. To my delight, six of them replied that they were coming and four were bringing a spouse or friend. (Due to travel plans, Vanda from Wyoming came a week earlier and Bianca from New Jersey a week later.)

From those who couldn't attend, I received an outpouring of congratulations and good wishes. As word of my labyrinth celebration spread among the community of women, packages began appearing in my mailbox, some quite heavy. Rocks, along with a handful of shells and one brick, were gifts—from their labyrinths to mine.

"Place this rock somewhere in your labyrinth," said a note tied to a large river rock. "As soon as I heard you were dedicating your labyrinth, I knew this rock was for you. Sending love and energy."

At eleven o'clock, we circled round the labyrinth holding hands. Fresh summer fragrances floated from nearby flowers and grass clippings. Shadowy outlines of leaves jumped playfully from one area of the labyrinth to another.

Ellie from Missouri sang an invocation as she faced each cardinal direction. Liz from New Mexico, Carolyn from Texas, Michele from Louisiana and Anne from Florida followed with poems and reflections. Linda from Ohio ended with words that spoke for all of us:

> "We have shown up today at this labyrinth dedication. By showing up, we are willing to step out of old paradigms (world views). We are willing to risk a new beginning. We are claiming our authority to take our place in this world and express ourselves. Every single person on this planet is on a powerful soul journey, whether they know it or not. May the richness of this day add to the richness of your soul."
>
> – Linda Landis

Granddaughter Ruby carried a bowl to the center and placed it gently on the grass. Each participant held a round wooden disk on which he/she had written an intention for the walk or a blessing for the labyrinth. They could keep the discs or place them in the bowl.

At the urging of everyone in the circle, I stepped into the labyrinth first. Ruby was a close second, followed by her mother (our daughter) Elizabeth who carried month-old Matthew in a carrier on her chest. Others chose to wander among the trees, sit on a bench, or wait around the labyrinth's edge until their turn to enter.

I paused on the outer ring in front of three Rose of Sharon shrubs. Their lowest amethyst flowers sheltered a miniature cairn. The base rock was one I had picked up on a walk with Marian around Walden Pond. I turned and found her, the friend who had traveled with me to seventeen states, kneeling beside the bowl in the center. She lightly placed her disc among the rest.

A smooth, white stone balanced precariously on top of the other two. The word JOURNEY, stamped in black letters, appeared across its width.

I nodded at its message and moved forward.

The Numbers

Two years.
Nineteen trips, grouped by criteria and geography.
Twenty-five trips alone.
Twenty-five with companions.
Ten car rentals.
Two private cars used ten times.
Fifty-six planes.
Thirty-eight hotels.
Three hundred sixteen cups of tea.
Four hundred thirty-one healthy snacks.
Five hundred eighty-seven unhealthy snacks
Zero accidents or lost luggage.
Miles? I lost count somewhere in New Mexico.
Infinite gratitude!

The author with one of her ten rental cars.

Labyrinth Resources

For a brief overview of labyrinths, consult Discover Labyrinths LLC (discoverlabyrinths.com/history) by Lars Howlett, professional labyrinth designer and builder.

World Wide Labyrinth Locator labyrinthlocator.com

A database which includes information about labyrinths you can visit in more than eighty countries. Currently the Labyrinth Locator contains approximately 5,200 labyrinths around the world. Information includes locations, contact details and types of labyrinths. Some entries provide photos. It is co-sponsored by The Labyrinth Society and Veriditas, Inc.

Refer to the World Wide Labyrinth Locator for specific details on the fifty women's labyrinths highlighted in this book. Each labyrinth is available for walking, except for Rhode Island and Vermont. In Elko, Nevada, the labyrinth at the Peace Park, which was designed by Sarah Sweetwater, is open to the public. Following her death, the contact information for her private labyrinth is no longer accurate.

The Labyrinth Society labyrinthsociety.org

A world-wide organization whose mission is to "support all those who create, maintain and use labyrinths and to serve the global community by providing education, networking and opportunities to experience transformation." Resources pages (labyrinthsociety.org/resources) provide a variety of educational materials.

Veriditas veriditas.org

A 501c3 nonprofit incorporated in California in 1995 by Lauren Artress. The word *Veriditas* originated with Hildegard of Bingen and means *the greening power of life.* Its mission is "to inspire personal and planetary change and renewal through the labyrinth experience." The organization accomplishes its mission by "training and supporting labyrinth facilitators around the world and offering meaningful events that promote further understanding of the labyrinth as a tool for personal and community transformation."

To locate a Veriditas-trained labyrinth facilitator, refer to the facilitator directory at www.veriditas.org/directory.

Suggested Guidelines for Walking a Labyrinth[1]

Quiet your mind and become aware of your breath. Allow yourself to find the pace your body wants to go. Since the path is two-way, those going in will meet those coming out. You may "pass" people or let others step around you. Do what feels natural. Walk the labyrinth with an open mind and an open heart.

Three stages of the walk:

- **Releasing** ~ A releasing, a letting go of the details of your life. This is the act of shedding thoughts and distractions. A time to open the heart and quiet the mind.
- **Receiving** ~ When you reach the center, stay there as long as you like. It is a place of meditation and prayer. Receive what is there for you to receive.
- **Returning** ~ As you follow the same path out of the center, you enter the third stage, which is joining God, your Higher Power, or the healing forces at work in the world. Each time you walk the labyrinth you become more empowered to find and do the work for which you feel your soul is reaching.

---

1. From Grace Cathedral, San Francisco, www.gracecathedral.org/our-labyrinths/.

Please keep in mind that there is no right (or wrong) way to walk a labyrinth. Walk, run, skip or dance at your own pace, in your own way. Your walk is between you and the labyrinth.

How to Draw a Classical, Seven-Circuit Labyrinth

In Gratitude

Although writing a book is primarily a solitary process, bringing it to life requires the writer to come up for air long enough to shout, "Help!" Thankfully, a community of family, friends and professionals rushed to my assistance.

Readers contributed long hours and insightful feedback. My only request was that they refrain from using red ink whenever possible. Memories of high school English are hard to shake.

Drew Alexander, Margie Beedle, Diane DeSloover, Anne Hornstein, Marian Levine, Jerry Mariah, Larry Patten, Beverly Racine, Kay Stolsonburg

Book and website designer and media consultant James Matthews. It is through James's broad range of talents and belief in my journey that this book is in your hands.

Artist Margie Beedle, whose original black and white sketches bring visual life to my written words. A friend and fellow labyrinth walker, Margie transforms the beauty of her native Juneau, Alaska into art that inspires the spirit and delights the senses.

Traveling companions, and dear friends, who accompanied me on half of my state visits. I now know how comforted Dorothy felt as she traveled to Oz with her three friends and Toto, too.

Margie Beedle, Marian Levine, Geri McLeod, Vivan Montoya, Mary Toland

The Reverend Dr. Lauren Artress, Founder and Creative Director of Veriditas, whose own labyrinth journey brought the labyrinth into my life and into the lives of countless others. This book, in fact my life's journey for the past five years, would never have occurred without her influence.

My family. Every journey begins from home, not necessarily from an actual house but—if you're lucky—from a person or persons who love you. I carried the love and unwavering support of my family across fifty states and two years of travel, followed by two years of writing. No matter where their own journeys take them, may they always know that my love is beside them, every step of the way.

Photo by Drew Alexander

Twylla Alexander stepped into her first labyrinth in 2004, unaware that labyrinths would lead her on a life-changing journey almost ten years later.

Traveling isn't new to her, having lived with her husband and three children in Arkansas, Alaska, Singapore, Cairo, Moscow and New York City. But a two-year journey to visit labyrinths and their creators, in all fifty states, was a personal pilgrimage.

Following retirement as a speech-language pathologist and elementary school teacher, Twylla has focused on her writing. She has blogged for seven years, most recently on New York City Reflections. Her writing has appeared in Lower Manhattan's *Downtown Magazine.*

Labyrinth Journeys: 50 States, 51 Stories is her first published book. She is a Veriditas-certified Labyrinth Facilitator and conducts labyrinth retreats, providing the space and time for women to explore their own journeys. Most mornings, you can find Twylla in her backyard, walking the labyrinth that she and her family created.

Learn more and contact her at **www.labyrinthjourneys.org**.

Made in the USA
San Bernardino, CA
03 February 2017